THEATRE

pres

C000202184

MAR~~~~
JOSIE
AND THE
CHINESE ELVIS

by

Charlotte Jones

faber and faber

'Celebrating 30 years at the forefront of British repertory theatre,' according to the *Manchester Evening News*, 'The Octagon really does have it all. It's glamorous but very friendly . . . production standards are very high and climbing. if you're not a regular, you should be.'

The Octagon Theatre was opened in November 1967 by Princess Margaret following the demolition of the last theatre in the town. Financial support from local individuals was matched by Bolton Council and the Arts Council for this revolutionary flexible theatre in which the auditorium could be changed from being 'in-the-round' to a more conventional 'end-on' relationship between stage and audience. The theatre seats between 364 and 420 people, depending upon the shape of the auditorium.

Existing as a full-time producing repertory theatre, The Octagon presents a varied programme of ten to twelve plays a year, embracing both British and international classic pieces, musicals, contemporary and new writing. The Bill Naughton Theatre was added in 1987, with a capacity of 70 to 100 seats, and stages not only Octagon productions throughout the year but also Youth Theatre workshops and productions. The Youth Theatre is part of Activ8 which was launched in September 1997 as The Octagon's Youth and Community programme.

The Octagon Theatre remains a true pioneer of innovative repertory theatre and the company seeks to maintain and surpass the hugely impressive standards that have already been achieved.

PRODUCTION CREDITS

for Martha, Josie and the Chinese Elvis

to Zebra Cards, St Andrews Court, Bolton, for birthday cards; to J. Sainsbury plc for vouchers; to K.P. Nuts for donation; to Janet Kay for bullwhip; to Magic Box for sunglasses; to Ikea for tent; to G.U.S.; to Revolution, Bolton, and Oscars, Bolton, for bottles; to B&Q, Bolton, for chain; to Haslam Moon, Bolton, for tissue paper; to Chris Raby at Superdrug for Wet Ones; to H.M.V. for loan of video

for Judging Billy Jones
to Strangeways Prison for food trays; and to Bolton Centre for Health

MARTHA, JOSIE
AND THE CHINESE ELVIS

by Charlotte Jones

MARTHA	Anny Tobin
JOSIE	Ann Rye
TIMOTHY WONG	Paul Courtenay Hyu
LIONEL	Malcolm Hebden
BRENDA-MARIE	Debra Penny
LOUISE	Melanie Ramsay

Directed by	Lawrence Till
Designed by	Dominie Hooper
Choreography	Lorelei Lynn
Lighting	Nick Johnson
Sound	Thomas Weir
DSM on the Book	Scott McDonald

Preview	Thursday 15 April 1999
Press Performance	Friday 16 April 1999
Final Performance	Saturday 8 May 1999

Charlotte Jones (Author)

Charlotte Jones read English at Oxford before becoming an actress. Her first play, *Airswimming*, was performed at the Battersea Arts Centre and was heard last year on Radio 4. Her second play, *In Flame*, has recently been a sell-out and critical success at the Bush Theatre, London. For the past year she has been writer-in-residence at the Octagon Theatre, Bolton, under the Pearson Television Theatre Writers' Scheme. She has written two more afternoon plays for Radio 4, *Mary Something takes the Veil* and *Future Perfect*, and is working on a fourth, *A Seer of Sorts*. She is also writing *Postcards* for Radio 4. *Martha, Josie and the Chinese Elvis* was awarded the Pearson Television Best Play Award in 1998. She is currently developing a series for Carlton TV and is under commission to Associated Capital Theatres.

Malcolm Hebden (Lionel)

Malcolm's wide theatre experience as an actor includes: *Feed* and *Just Between Ourselves* at the Stephen Joseph Theatre, Scarborough; *The Crucible* and *Pravda* at Leeds Playhouse; *Twelfth Night* at Oldham Coliseum; *The Seagull* and *What the Butler Saw* at the Duke's Playhouse, Lancaster; *Harvey* at the Royal Exchange; *All In Good Time*, *Gaslight* and *Road* at the Octagon, Bolton; *Sweeney Todd* and *Privates on Parade* at the Redgrave, Farnham; *The Rivals* and *Endgame* at Liverpool Playhouse; and *The Birthday Party*, *A Midsummer Night's Dream* and *Fool for Love* at Contact, Manchester. He has had a long association with Alan Ayckbourn at the Stephen Joseph Theatre in Scarborough where he has appeared in over ten world premières and was also an Associate Director. Malcolm's many television credits include *Coronation Street* for Granada in which he played Norris

Cole, *A Bit of a Do* (two series), *Heartbeat* and *Stay Lucky* for
Yorkshire TV, *Spyship* and *Juliet Bravo* for the BBC and *Spoils of
War, Sherlock Holmes, Band of Gold, Albion Market, In Suspicious
Circumstances* and *The Rik Mayall Playhouse* for Granada.
He broadcasts regularly on Radio 4 both in plays and reading the
'Morning Story'. As well as acting, Malcolm is also an experienced
theatre director and has recently directed *Dead Funny* at Oldham
Coliseum, where he also did *The Cemetery Club.*

Paul Courtenay Hyu
(Timothy Wong)

Paul was born in London and was
brought up in Harrogate. Theatre work
includes *Hiawatha at* the Royal Lyceum,
Edinburgh, *The Merchant of Venice* at
the Sherman Theatre, Cardiff, *Cinderella*
at the Arts Theatre, *The Wind in the
Willows* at the Old Vic, Miss Saigon at
the Theatre Royal, Drury Lane, *Three
Japanese Women* at the Cockpit Theatre.
His family moved *to* Germany in 1977
and he speaks fluent German. Paul
has appeared in *M. Butterfly* at the Deutsches Schauspielhaus in
Hamburg and in *Titus Andronicus* in Cologne. Other theatre work
includes *The Magic Fundoshi* and *The Fantasticks* in Singapore and
New Territories in Hong Kong as well as tours with White Horse
Theatre and Carib Theatre companies. TV work includes *Bugs,
One Foot in the Grave, Comedy Nation, TVK, Doctor at the Top*
and *The Blackheath Poisonings.* He can be seen regularly on
Germany's RTL TV in the series *Echt Harder,* set in Hamburg.
Radio work includes *Fifteen-Love, Devils in the Glass, Black Walls,
The Adventures of Tin-Tin* and *Prize-Giving.* Film work includes
The Nightwatch, The First Nine and a Half Weeks, and the soon to
be released *Wing Commander* and *Everybody Loves Sunshine.*
Paul is artistic director of Mu-Lan Theatre Company, the country's
premiere British–Oriental theatre company, whose production of
Takeaway, which Paul helped to devise, is currently on tour and will
be playing shortly at the Library Theatre, Manchester, and the
Everyman, Liverpool. He has also recently written for and directed
the country's first British–Oriental comedy revue, *Mu-Lan's Frying
Circus,* which premiered at Canary Wharf in February as part of the
Yan Huang International Chinese Arts Festival.

Debra Penny (Brenda-Marie)

Debra trained at Manchester Polytechnic
School of Drama. She has recently
appeared at the Festival of Visual
Theatre, Battersea Arts Centre, in
Bitching, Boozing and Bumming Fags,
and at the Library Theatre, Manchester,
in *The Snow Queen*. Debra has worked
extensively in the north and northwest,
especially at the Octagon Theatre,
Bolton, playing various roles in
A Christmas Carol, Dull Gret and Angie
in *Top Girls* and Angela in *Abigail's
Party*, and at Harrogate Theatre in *Second from Last in the Sack
Race* as Aunty Doris. Other theatre includes *A Midsummer Night's
Dream* (Hermia/Starveling), *Hansel and Gretel* and *Criminals in
Love*, all at Contact Theatre, Manchester, *Enter The Clown* for
Company Paradiso, *The Weavers* at the Gate Theatre, London, and
Twelfth Night and *The Merchant of Venice* at Liverpool Playhouse.
Debra has also appeared in a number of European tours for English
Teaching Theatre, and has played countless roles in both Northwest
Playwrights and Young Playwrights Festivals at Contact Theatre.
She has also appeared in television in *East Enders*, *The Bill*, *London
Bridge, Families, The Krypton Factor*, *First of the Summer Wine*
and *Medics*. Radio work includes *The End of the World Was the Best
Thing that Ever Happened to Me, Stolen Kisses* and *Boomerang* for
Radio 4.

Melanie Ramsay (Louise)

Melanie trained at the Guildhall School
of Music and Drama and was last seen
at the Octagon in Edward Bond's *Saved*
in 1998. Recent theatre credits include
Communicating Doors and *Time of Your
Life* at the Library Theatre, Manchester,
Northanger Abbey and *As You Like It*
at the Mercury Theatre, *The Importance
of Being Earnest* at the Royal Exchange,
Bare at Oldham Coliseum and *A Patriot
for Me* for the Royal Shakespeare
Company. Melanie has been seen on

television in *The Bill*, *Birds of a Feather*, *The Rector's Wife*, *House of Elliott*, *Castles*, *No Child of Mine* and *A Touch of Frost*. Film work includes appearances in Kenneth Branagh's *Hamlet* and Dennis Potter's *Midnight Movie*.

Ann Rye (Josie)

Ann trained at Morley College and the Webber-Douglas Academy. Her theatre credits include the National Theatre, the Royal Court Theatre and the West End, as well as theatres all over the country. She has also appeared in many TV soaps and dramas, from *A Farewell to Arms* and *St Joan* to the original *Dr Finlay's Casebook* and *Coronation Street*. Her film credits include *Wide-Eyed and Legless*, *Don't Look Now* and *Final Exit*. She was a member of Granada's unique Stables Theatre/TV Company, and wrote and presented her own slot in ATV's *Women Today*. Ann has done extensive work for radio, including stories, plays, religious programmes and serials – the latest being *Joseph Andrews*. More recent theatre work has been at the Bristol Old Vic, the Derby Playhouse, and at the Octagon in *Fastest Clock in the Universe*, *Derby Day*, *Talking Heads* (*A Cream Cracker under the Settee*) and *Ghost from a Perfect Place* – both award-winning performances.

Anny Tobin (Martha)

Anny last appeared at the Octagon in 1998 in Samuel Beckett's *Happy Days*, for which she won the Best Actress award from the Manchester Evening News. In 1996, she was seen here in Alan Bennett's *Talking Heads 2*, playing Susan in *Bed Among the Lentils*, and Beatrice in *View from the Bridge*. She may also be remembered as Fraulein Schneider in *Cabaret* in 1993. Recent theatre elsewhere includes Mother Peter in a national tour of *Once a Catholic* and

Anna Pavlovna in *War and Peace* at the Royal National Theatre. Other London work includes Pam in *Our Own Kind* at the Bush, Mrs Hudetz in *Judgement Day* at the Old Red Lion, Doris in *Don't You Call Me Anything but Mother* at the Mermaid, and Kate in *Dancing at Lughnasa* at the Garrick, for which she was nominated as Best Actress in the 1992 TMA Regional Theatre Awards. Anny's regional work includes many plays at Chester Gateway (Kate Keller in *All My Sons*, Beverly in *Abigail's Party*, Mrs Kendal in *The Elephant Man*), Liverpool Playhouse (Nell in *Passion Play*, Helen in *A Taste of Honey*), the Duke's, Lancaster (Esther in *The Price*), the Northcott in Exeter (Judith Bliss in *Hay Fever* and Joanne in Sondheim's *Company*), Derby Playhouse, Sheffield Crucible, Farnham and Harrogate. Anny's TV and film credits include roles in *Angels, Lifelike, Shadow of a Noose, Brookside, Soldier, Soldier, Wycliffe, Milner, Peak Practice* and *The Fifteen Streets* (Mary-Ellen O'Brien). During the last year she was seen in the film *Monk Dawson*, and in TV's *Casualty, Grafters* and *Holby City*. Recent radio work include's *The Pig's Back* (BBC Radio 2), *Dream of Spring, The Donahue Sisters* and a short story entitled *In Smoke Concealed*, all for BBC Radio 4.

Lawrence Till (Director)

Lawrence has been Artistic Director and Chief Executive of the Octagon Theatre, Bolton, since 1991. He directed the world premières of *Feed, Possession, The Resurrectionists* and *The Rough Side of the Boards*, and a new translation by Henry Livings of Lorca's *Blood Wedding*. His adaptations include Bill Naughton's *Derby Day* and *Annie and Fanny from Bolton to Rome*, Barry Hines' *Kes*, and *Pat and Margaret* by Victoria Wood. His interpretation of Shakespeare's *Titus Andronicus*, integrating deaf and hearing actors, was described by the Arts Council of Great Britain as a landmark production and was the recipient of their Be Bold Award and a Bolton Evening News Outstanding Achievement Award. His production of Philip Ridley's *The Fastest Clock in the Universe* won Best Production of a Play in the 1995 Manchester Evening News Awards, and he was nominated for Best Director in the 1995 Theatrical Management Association British Regional Theatre Awards, and again in 1997 for Caryl Churchill's *Top Girls*. Other productions he has directed at the Octagon include *Alfie, The Pocket Dream, The Suicide, Talking Heads, Macbeth, La Mandragola, The Rise and Fall of Little Voice, The Ghost Train, Edward the Second, The Pitchfork Disney, Ghost from a Perfect Place*, and *Saved*. He was previously Youth Director and later Associate Director at Contact Theatre, Manchester, and Education Director at the Crucible Theatre in Sheffield. Lawrence's other productions include *A Passionate*

Woman (Oldham Coliseum, Redgrave Theatre, Farnham), *The Snow Queen* (Theatr Clwyd), *The Red Balloon* and *The Dinner Party* (Contact Theatre), *Private Times* (Library Theatre), *Whale, Binnin' It* and *Joyriders* (nominated for TMA Best Play for Children and Young People) at the Crucible Theatre, Sheffield. He is Series Editor of Heinemann Plays and is on the Boards of North West Playwrights and the National Council for Drama Training.

Dominie Hooper (Designer)

After graduating from Nottingham University with a First Class Hons Degree in Theatre Design, Dominie has enjoyed a wealth of highly acclaimed work. She designed the Octagon Youth Theatre production of *Hamlet* in the Bill Naughton Theatre, and their production *of Pallingo* for Streets Ahead Festival. Last season, Dominie designed Paines Plough's *Northern Exposure* for the Bill Naughton Theatre, and in the main house D. H. Lawrence's *The Daughter-in-Law*, *The Mikado* (co-design), Jim Cartwright's *Two*, and Victoria Wood's *Pat and Margaret*. Other theatre work includes productions with Cardboard Citizens, Roundabout Theatre Company, Pop Up Theatre and Theatre Centre. Touring work includes, with Theatre Alibi, *The Goose, The Pales, Sarawak, Birthday, All at Sea, Little White Lies, Fly by Night, Sea of Faces* and *The Night before Christmas* (in collaboration with the RSC). Film and TV credits include costume work on *She's Out* for Cinema Variety, *Wings of the Dove* for Bridgewater Films, *A Question of Guilt* for BBC Films – and the Dettox advert with David Bellamy.

Lorelei Lynn (Choreography)

Lorelei trained at the Bush Davies School. She first choreographed The Who's rock opera *Tommy*, and has since worked extensively throughout the country. Amongst her many credits are: *Women Beware Women, The Relapse, Privates on Parade* and *The Wizard of Oz*, all for the Birmingham Repertory Theatre; *The Red Balloon* for Contact Theatre, Manchester, and Bristol Old Vic Company; *The Three Musketeers* and *The Wonderful World of the Brothers Grimm* for the Northcott, Exeter; *Romeo and Juliet* for Temba Theatre Company at the Young Vic; and *Into the Woods, A Midsummer Night's Dream* and *Love's Labours Lost* at the Wolsey Theatre, Ipswich. She worked on the *York Cycle of Mystery Plays*, and returned to York for *Jane Eyre*. She has worked extensively at the Octagon, Bolton, and recently choreographed *Feed, The Suicide, Mowgu's Jungle, Kes! the Musical, A Midsummer Night's Dream, The Nativity, A View from the Bridge, Cabaret, Dancing at Lughnasa* and *Talent*. At Cheltenham's Everyman she recently choreographed *And a Nightingale Sang* and *A Little Shop of Horrors* and for Derby Playhouse *Tess of the D'Urbervilles* and *The Rise and Fall of Little Voice*. For the Park at Lancaster Lorelei choreographed *A Midsummer Night's Dream*, *The Three Musketeers* and most recently *Alice's Adventures in Wonderland*. She has choreographed two television specials for Television South.

Nick Johnson (Lighting Designer)

Nick studied theatre production and lighting design at Croydon College. Since then he has worked extensively within the theatre industry, in a variety of venues from the Gardner Arts Centre in Brighton to the nationally renowned Crucible Theatre in Sheffield. More recently he was lighting designer on several open-air productions (in all weathers!) for the Duke's, Lancaster, including *Cyrano do Bergerac*, *The Importance of Being Earnest* and *Comedy of Errors*. Nick has also worked as sound designer for many repertory productions, including *Neville's Island*, *The Snow Queen* and *Great Expectations*. Since Nick became Lighting Designer at the Octagon he has worked on *Pat and Margaret* and *How the Other Half Loves*.

Thomas Weir (Sound Designer)

Before joining the Octagon, Thomas worked as Deputy Chief Electrician at the Pitlochry Festival in Scotland for three years, becoming Chief Electrician for the 1998 season. As a sound designer he has worked on a diverse range of productions, including *Travels With My Aunt*, *Don't Dress for Dinner* in the West End, and the Scottish première of *Funny Money* by Ray Cooney. Prior to his sojourn in Scotland, Tom had worked with Channel Theatre Company, M6 Theatre Company and at Buxton Opera House, as well as touring as lighting designer with Action Transport Theatre Company.

Scott McDonald (DSM on the Book)

Having given up working in circus, Scott has worked for TAG, Glasgow; Traverse Theatre, Edinburgh; Contact and the Royal Exchange, Manchester; West Yorkshire Playhouse, Leeds; the Lyric, Hammersmith; and Hull Truck. Fun shows include *Sunset Song*, *A Clockwork Orange*, *Tom Sawyer*, *The Fall of the House of Usher*, *Wolk's World*, *Hooray for Hollywood*, *Mill on the Floss*, *The Wasp Factory*, *Happy Days* and *The Wizard of Oz*. Scott also taught stage management at Arden College, Manchester. Unfortunately, Scott is soon to leave us to become a private eye.

OCTA8ON THEATRE BOLTON

THEATRE STAFF

ADMINISTRATION

Artistic Director and Chief Executive	**Lawrence Till**
Administrative Director	**Amanda Belcham**
Assistant Administrator	**Christine Cunningham**
Finance Officer	**Ian Muschamp**
Resident Playwright	**Charlotte Jones**
activ8 Director	**Sue Reddish**
activ8 Youth Theatre Leader	**Jason Anders**
activ8 Outreach Worker	**Pete Smith**
activ8 Administration Assistant	**Caroline Gleaves**

MARKETING AND SALES

Head of Marketing and Sales	**Lynn Melville**
Press and Marketing Officer	**Rachel Bartholomew**
Ticket Sales Manager	**Marie Irving-Murphy**
Ticket Sales Staff	**Frances Shinks, Edward Hamer, Christian Lisseman Dawn Barlow, Julie Dodd, Caroline Gleaves**
Stage Door Receptionist	**Nicola Hallmark**

FRONT OF HOUSE

House Manager	**Ann Marie Westmoreland**
Duty House Manager	**Caroline Gleaves**
BNT House Manager	**Barbara Irving**
FOH Staff	**Jane Alker, Elizabeth Harrison, Barbara Irving, Brian Kearney, Philip Hussey, Shona Ingram, Robert Thoday, Anna Ferguson, Emma Fearnley, Gareth Round, Cathy Atkinson, Deborah Knowles, Helen Crosbie, Fiona Tatterton and members of activ8**
Senior Cleaner	**June Brown**
Cleaners	**Joanne Brookfield, Colin Foster, Barbara Lord**

TECHNICAL STAFF

Production Manager	**Jim Niblett**
Production Assistant	**Clare Lewis**
Resident Designer	**Richard Wood**
Scenic Artist	**Michael Roberts**
Stage Manager	**Kim Wiltshire**
Deputy Stage Managers	**Scott McDonald, Jackie Bell**
Assistant Stage Manager	**Andrina Van Den Berg**
Chief Electrician	**Nick Johnson**
Deputy Chief Electrician	**Thomas Weir**
Assistant Carpenter	**Darren Garner**
Wardrobe Supervisor	**Mary Horan**
Deputy Wardrobe Supervisor	**Anita Bateson**
Wardrobe Maintenance	**Pauline Baker**

BAR AND CATERING STAFF

Licensed Bar Manager	**John Walker**
Deputy Bar Manage	**Ajay C Dhodakia**
Bar Staff	**Linda Boddy, Janet Holloway, S J Hughes**
	M Mackay, L Russell, Anne Whaite, James Whaite

SPOTLIGHT CAFE

Catering Manager	**Jane Barber**
Deputy Catering Manager	**Carol Brown**
Catering Staff	**Janet Meehan, Nazma Omerjee**
	Sarah Povey, Christine McLaren, Kelly Cox

The Theatre has the support of the Pearson Television Writers' Scheme
sponsored by The Mackintosh Foundation

Thanks to Business in the Arts:North West
for their continued training support

ACKNOWLEDGEMENTS FOR THE SEASON
Wardrobe care courtesy of ACDO. Torches and batteries courtesy of Ever Ready.
Thanks also to Bolton Central Library, T J Stokes (Opticians),
The Sue Ryder Shop. Physiotherapy provided by Karen Willcock,
Bolton Therapy Centre, 13 Chorley Old Road, Bolton (01204 386170).
Kirkby Central for transport and APCOA Car Park.
Dry Cleaning by Faddies (0161 928 7660)

Investing in the Arts

Charlotte Jones
Martha, Josie
and the Chinese Elvis

faber and faber

First published in 1999
by Faber and Faber Limited
3 Queen Square, London WC1N 3AU

Typeset by Country Setting, Kingsdown, Kent CT14 8ES
Printed in England by Intype London Ltd

A CIP record for this book
is available from the British Library

ISBN 0–571–20237–3

4 6 8 10 9 7 5 3

Characters

Brenda-Marie Botting

Martha Clear

Josie Botting

Lionel Trills

The Chinese Elvis (Timothy Wong)

Louise

Act One

SCENE ONE

*We are in Josie Botting's front room. It is a respectable
lower middle-class front room – perhaps it's still a bit
seventies in décor, but not tatty. There are Christmas
decorations up. Brenda-Marie probably put these up, so
they are rather gaudy and uncoordinated. The decorations
look tired. There are four exits: one to the front door,
sliding glass doors that lead to the patio and garden, an
exit that leads to the kitchen and one that leads upstairs.
There is a window with net curtains. There are one or
two family photographs – not excessive – which show
Josie with her two daughters – Brenda-Marie and Shelly-
Louise. There is a mirror on one wall. It is 6 January
(Feast of Epiphany).*

Music: Elvis Presley, 'Suspicion'.

*Brenda-Marie is a podgy young woman of about
thirty, with learning difficulties. Brenda-Marie leans
against the window staring out. Perhaps she blows
against the frame and writes the word SNOW on the
window. Then she rips up pieces of tissue paper to make
'snow'.*

*She pays no attention as Martha Clear enters the living
room. She is an Irish woman in her mid-forties with
very long hair (in a plait down her back) and obsessive-
compulsive disorder. She comes through the door, shuts
it and turns the handle five times.*

Martha *(under her breath)* One, two, three, four, five.

Brenda-Marie Snow.

Martha then taps the door in sequence from the top.

Martha One, two, three, four, five.

Brenda-Marie Please God.

Martha repeats the sequence.

Martha One, two, three, four, five.

Brenda-Marie Please snow.

She throws the pieces of tissue paper into the air. The music starts to fade. Martha gets out her cleaning utensils ready to start work. Again her movements are very ritualistic.

Martha Look at this mess. One, two, three, four, five. One, two, three, four, five. One, two, three, four, five. In the name of the Father, Son and Holy Ghost.

Brenda-Marie Come on God, snow! We want some snow. Bloody well snow, God!

Martha It's too cold to snow.

Brenda-Marie gives Martha a black look. Martha starts to polish the furniture. Her counting is in rhythm to her cleaning.

Martha One, two, three, four, five. One, two, three, four, five.

Brenda-Marie Six! Six! Six!

Martha (*covers her ears*) No! No! You evil girl. Get away from me.

She returns to the first point that she was polishing. Frantically she begins again.

Martha One, two, three, four, five.

Brenda-Marie You're a nutter, Holy Jo. You always forget the six. One, two, three, four, five, SIX! Even I know that.

Martha Get away from me, child of Satan. One, two, three, four, five –

Brenda-Marie Six.

Martha No that's not right. I'll have to start all over again. One, two, three, four, five –

Brenda-Marie (*she whispers it this time*) Six.

Martha (*ignores her*) That's better. Yes. Un, deux, trois, quatre, cinq –

Brenda-Marie (*she shouts delightedly in French*) Six, Holy Jo, six!

Martha If you say that particular number one more time, I shall scalp you.

Brenda-Marie Sorry, Holy Jo.

Martha And don't call me that. R301 VOY. Yes. E953 HAV. Yes. F148 PBH. Yes. Yes. Yes.

Brenda-Marie What you saying now, Holy Jo?

Martha The number plates. I remembered all the suspicious looking number-plates on the way here.

Brenda-Marie Number-plates?

Martha On the cars. The suspicious looking cars on the way here.

Brenda-Marie Why were they suspicious?

Martha Crime is rife, Brenda-Marie. You have to be on the lookout for suspicious individuals.

Brenda-Marie And suspicious-looking cars?

Martha Exactly.

Brenda-Marie What did they look like?

Martha One was blue and two were red. But it was more the number-plates that gave them away. Those number-plates spoke volumes to me. But then I've a trained eye.

Brenda-Marie You should be a detective, Holy Jo instead of me Mam's cleaner.

Martha Brenda-Marie. In this world today evil is everywhere. Evil is always about to happen. It's imminent. And from the most unexpected quarters. On the way here while I was collecting my number-plate data, I was almost run over by an emergency ambulance. Would you credit it? But then I've always maintained that these paramedics are seldom to be trusted. One, two, three, four, five. And all that's as nothing compared to the incident of evil involving my kettle.

Brenda-Marie (*bored*) Yes, Holy Jo.

Martha My life savings were in that kettle.

Brenda-Marie I know. But what I don't understand is why did you keep your life savings in a kettle, Holy Jo?

Martha I never drink hot beverages. Hot beverages are an invitation to Satan.

Brenda-Marie What's his favourite?

Martha What?

Brenda-Marie Satan. I bet he likes cappucino. I like cappucino.

Martha One, two, three, four, five. I'm not speaking to you, evil girl.

Brenda-Marie Why did you have a kettle then, Holy Jo? If you don't drink hot drinks?

Martha In case of emergency.

Brenda-Marie What sort of emergency?

Martha I don't know. In case a child was about to be born in the vicinity.

Brenda-Marie Why do you need hot water then?

Martha To prevent contamination.

Brenda-Marie What sort of contamination?

Martha One, two, three, four, five. Now don't rile me, Brenda-Marie. I had a kettle because it was a cunning place in which to keep my life savings. What do you expect to find in a kettle, Brenda-Marie?

Brenda-Marie Water, Holy Jo.

Martha Yes. Exactly.

Brenda-Marie And lime-scale.

Martha Precisely.

Brenda-Marie And the element.

Martha (*impatiently*) Yes all right. But, ha, ha, who would expect to find four hundred pounds in a kettle? I ask you that.

Brenda-Marie The robber who nicked yours.

Martha That was a sore day for me, Brenda-Marie. To discover that my kettle had been ransacked. I felt violated, I don't mind telling you.

Brenda-Marie You should have put the money in the bank. Me Mam has all our money in the bank.

Martha Banks are not to be trusted any more, Brenda-Marie.

Brenda-Marie Neither are kettles.

Martha Do you know what I was going to do with that money, Brenda-Marie?

Brenda-Marie Yes, Holy Jo.

Martha I was going to fly to Graceland. To see where my King is buried. Memphis, Tennessee. What a beautiful sound those words have. Do you know what those words conjure for me, Brenda-Marie?

Brenda-Marie No, Holy Jo.

Martha Peace. They conjure up peace to me.

Brenda-Marie I thought you were going to go to Lourdes where they throw all the sick Catholics in the holy water.

Martha Of course I was hoping to include Lourdes in my itinerary. And they don't throw them in. They dip them in.

Brenda-Marie Like chicken nuggets.

Martha Yes something like that . . . Nothing would have stopped me, Brenda-Marie. A pilgrimage to Graceland . . . hopefully taking in the healing waters of Lourdes on the way back.

Brenda-Marie And now you're going nowhere. You're staying in Farnworth and being me and me Mam's cleaner.

Martha I made a big mistake when I came over to England. I got on that train with my ticket to Bolton. But then I saw those fateful words: 'Moses Gate'. And I thought, this is the place for me. What on earth was I thinking of? I should have got off at Lostock. Nothing happens in Moses Gate. Not so much as a burning bush.

Brenda-Marie Why don't you cut your hair, Holy Jo?

Martha Questions, questions, nothing but questions from you. Bad girl. Don't you see I have a job to do?

SCENE TWO

She returns to polishing. During this Josie, Brenda-Marie's mother enters. She's absently looking at the post. She deposits it on the mantle.

Martha One, two, three, four, five.

Brenda-Marie What would happen if you didn't count, Holy Jo?

Josie Don't be pestering Miss Clear now, Brenda-Marie. Not when she's working.

Martha Do you want me to take these decorations down, Mrs Botting?

Brenda-Marie No, leave them Mam.

Martha They have to come down today.

Brenda-Marie Last year we didn't take them down till February.

Josie We'll do it later, Miss Clear.

Martha Very well. Then I thought I might wash the walls today, Mrs Botting.

Josie There's no need, Miss Clear.

Martha Then the carpets. I could wash the carpets.

Josie That's too big a job for one day.

Martha Well, I'll definitely do all the tops of the doors.

Josie Very well.

Brenda-Marie She loves cleaning, our cleaner, doesn't she Mam?

Martha And I could spring clean all the kitchen cupboards?

Brenda-Marie It's not Spring yet, Holy Jo. It's still winter. It's going to snow soon.

Martha At least let me bleach the bin. I'd feel much happier if I could do that. And wax the kitchen floor.

Josie You can do the bin.

Martha And I noticed the brass needs polishing.

Josie Miss Clear, you're on an hourly rate. You'll have me bankrupt.

Martha (*close to tears*) It's not the money! I want to do it! Just let me do it! I just want it all right, Mrs Botting.

Josie We really can't have this battle every day, Miss Clear. I am very happy with your work but you mustn't get excessive.

Brenda-Marie You've missed a bit over here, Holy Jo.

Martha (*rushes over*) You put this smear here. It definitely wasn't here before. One, two, three, four, five. I'll have to start over now. Right from the beginning.

Josie That's it, Brenda-Marie. You naughty girl. You mustn't torment Miss Clear like that. Miss Clear, leave it please. I appreciate your diligence but the thing is I've got a client coming over shortly.

Martha Oh. I see.

Josie You can do an extra long shift at the beginning of next week.

Martha No, no. I don't want your pity, Mrs Botting. I've quite enough to do with ridding my own flat of germs.

Brenda-Marie Holy Jo lives in a germy flat.

Josie Brenda-Marie! I do need a few things from the shops, Miss Clear. I wondered if you'd go for me.

Martha (*suspiciously*) How many things?

Josie Just one or two.

Martha How much will it come to?

Josie Under five pounds.

Martha It's just that certain numbers – I won't be able to buy it, if it comes to certain numbers.

Josie Of course, Miss Clear. I understand. Just do your best. My client will be here for about an hour, for his counselling session –

Martha I see.

Josie That's right. So we mustn't be disturbed for an hour.

Brenda-Marie My Mam counsels all and sundry. But mostly sundry. (*She giggles.*)

Josie Brenda-Marie.

Brenda-Marie You're all at me. All the time. You're all on at me.

Josie Bren, love –

Brenda-Marie I wish my sister wasn't dead, then I could have someone my own age to play. with. Shelly-Louise never went on at me.

Martha (*crosses herself*) God rest her soul.

Josie Brenda, don't talk about Shelly-Louise. Not today.

Brenda-Marie Why can't I talk about her? She's my sister. Just because she's dead. She's still my sister.

She runs upstairs. Josie takes the post from the mantle and sits down heavily.

Martha A Mother's loss is always the worst, Mrs Botting.

Josie Yes, yes.

Martha I'd better get going then.

Josie (*looking at the cards*) It's my birthday, Miss Clear. I'm sixty today.

Martha Many happy returns, Mrs Botting.

Josie Oh, I don't think so.

Martha What?

Josie I think I've had enough happy returns. Off you go anyway. I've left the money and the list by your bag. Don't rush. Have a cup of tea in Whittakers if you want.

Martha I never drink tea, Mrs Botting.

Josie Oh no, of course.

Martha And I try to avoid foreign cups if at all possible. You can never be too careful.

Josie No.

Martha I'll pop back in just over an hour.

Josie That's right, Miss Clear.

Martha goes to the door, she knocks five times (a bit more surreptitiously this time) and turns the knob five times

Martha One, two, three, four, five. Sorry about this Mrs Botting.

Josie You go ahead.

Martha repeats the whole ritual at double quick speed and exits very speedily

Martha One, two, three, four, five. Goodbye, Mrs Botting. (*She exits.*)

Josie Bye now, Miss Clear. Don't step on the cracks. Like I have all me life.

Josie arranges her one or two cards (she tries to spread them out perhaps).
Brenda-Marie comes back in.

Brenda-Marie Sorry, Mam.

Josie That's all right, pet.

Brenda-Marie Did you like me card?

Josie Beautiful, pet.

Josie sits back down.

Brenda-Marie I thought I might practise me ice-dancin' for you.

Josie I just want a little rest before Lionel comes, love.

Brenda-Marie I'll do it quiet, Mam.

Josie All right, love.

Josie shuts her eyes. Brenda-Marie goes over to the window and perches on the ledge – her commentary box. Perhaps she takes a brass poker from the fireplace to use as a microphone. She speaks quietly at first and then gets carried away. She doesn't move during her commentary – she is imagining it.

Brenda-Marie And here we are in the Olympic Stadium in Heidelburger. It's snowing outside. (*She gestures outside.*) Brrrr. And onto the rink come our first contestants. Here they are, Brenda-Marie and Shelly-Louise

Botting, the sisters from Bolton. Tonight they're skating for (*She pauses.*) – Canada. As Brenda-Marie told us earlier they didn't want to skate for Britain because then they were bound to come fifteenth because after Torvill and Dean all the British couples come fifteenth and Barry Davies says they've made a very good effort when really they haven't, they've been shit and landed on their bum loads of times.

Josie (*she doesn't open her eyes*) Brenda-Marie!

Brenda-Marie Sorry Mam . . . Shelly-Louise and Brenda-Marie are in top position after their short programme where they completed all their compulsory elements with ease. We're all very much looking forward to their free programme. They're skating to a medley of Elvis songs. Brenda-Marie has promised us they're going to attempt a flying split triple twist. If anyone can do it these girls from Bolton can.

The doorbell goes. It is the first few bars of 'Love Me Tender'.

Josie I'll go love. (*She rouses herself from the chair and makes her way to the front door.*)

Brenda-Marie And they're skating perfectly together. Brenda-Marie has stronger technique but Shelly-Louise is a lovely expressive little skater. See her launch like a rocket into the air in that triple twist.

We hear Josie greet Lionel offstage.
Josie enters with Lionel, a short, dapper, balding but kindly looking man of about fifty.

Lionel Hello there, Brenda-Marie.

Josie Say hello to Lionel, Brenda-Marie.

Brenda-Marie I'm in the middle of a routine, Mam.

Lionel I'll go straight up and get changed then. Back in a jiffy.

Josie The thing is Lionel, I don't know if I'm up to it today. I'm very tired.

Brenda-Marie Mammy's very tired.

Lionel You know me, Josie. I don't want anything too energetic.

Josie It takes a lot out of me, Lionel. I don't think I've got the strength.

Lionel Well look, since I've come all this way, why don't we just have a quick session and if you want to stop at any time, we will.

Josie Oh all right, Lionel. You drive a hard bargain. I'll show you up.

Lionel and Josie exit.

Brenda-Marie Now Brenda-Marie lifts her high in an inverted star lift. Delightful landing into the triple lutz. Low into the triple salcho. Side-by-side triple toe loop. Now the laid-back spin into the camel spin. These girls are really doing Bolton and Canada proud. And now for the finale. Flying split triple twist. Brenda-Marie flies fifteen feet accross the ice. In her multicoloured dress she flashes across the ice like a rainbow. A human rainbow! And she's coming into land now. Will she hold onto it? Yes! The landing's good. The crowd's on its feet. The judge from the Ukraine is crying. These sisters are so good. And there they hold up the marks. Marks for technical merit. Six from the US of A. Yes! Six from Hungary. Six from Australia and New Zealand and the Isle of Man. But oh no! Five point nine from the Belarusse. The crowd's up in arms. They're booing, they're jeering, they're attacking the Belarusse lady. Silly

17

cow. She deserves it. She's like Holy Jo. She never gives us six.

Josie enters again.

The Belarusse only gave us five point nine, Mammy.

Josie Ahh! Never mind, love. You'll have to let Mammy work now, Brenda-Marie.

Brenda-Marie I know, I know. I'm going to my tent.

Josie Don't get cold.

Brenda-Marie I never get cold, Mam.

Josie Off you go then.

Brenda-Marie runs outside. Josie looks around the room. Perhaps she straightens a Christmas decoration. She takes some deep breaths. The door knocks. Her demeanour changes sharply.

I can't hear you. Use a firm hand.

Lionel knocks again.

Yes?

Lionel's voice from behind the door.

Lionel May I come in, Madam Josie?

Josie Who is it?

Lionel It is I, Miss Geraldine.

Josie Ah, Geraldine. You'd better show yourself then. Let me give you the once over.

Lionel enters, wearing a French maid's outfit.

You forgot to curtsy, Miss Geraldine.

Lionel Oh I do beg your utmost pardon, Madam Josie.

He curtsies.

Josie Lower, Miss Geraldine. I cannot abide a sloppy curtsy.

Lionel Sorry, Madam.

Josie You will anger your Madam, Miss Geraldine. Follow the form, young lady, or Madam Josie will be forced to wreak havoc upon you.

Lionel Yes, Madam.

Lionel Will that entail your cuffing equipment?

Josie It may well do, Miss Geraldine. Although you are presumptious in assuming to comment upon your Madam's preferred method of punishing tool.

Lionel Of course, Madam. You bend over backwards for us girls, Madam.

Josie Yes, but do I get a word of thanks?

Lionel I think I always show my gratitude, madam.

Josie Don't be cocky, Miss Geraldine. It doesn't suit you.

Lionel No Madam.

Josie Now let's have less of the lip and more of the action from you.

Lionel Do you wish me to adopt slave position, Madam?

Josie No, no. Today since it's my sixtieth birthday, you're going to get off lightly.

Lionel May I be the first to congratulate you on your birthday, Madam? And may I be so bold as to enquire whether in spite of this great anniversary you'll still find it in your heart to beat me with a paddle?

Josie If you're very lucky. Oh yes, when I've finished with you, you'll need more than a few tubs of lanolin. But first I need you to dust my ornamentation.

Lionel Of course.

Josie Begin, Geraldine, and let your Madam observe.

He takes out a feather duster, begins to dust some ornaments on the mantelpiece.

Josie Petticoat, Geraldine.

Lionel Is it slipping, Madam?

Josie A bad case of subsidence where your undergarments are concerned I fear, Geraldine.

Lionel Am I a slut, Madam?

Josie You know what you are, Geraldine.

Lionel Almost definitely a slut.

Josie A nice girl is always in control of her gusset, Miss Geraldine. I shall have to consider how best to remedy this situation.

Lionel Whatever you think, Madam.

Josie I think a swift course of treatment may be necessary.

Lionel Involving?

Josie Involving all sorts of disciplinary procedures.

Lionel Would you like to give me some idea of what they might be, Madam?

Josie No. I would not.

Lionel Oh, Josie!

Josie I told you when you came Lionel, I'm not really feeling up to it today.

Lionel But you were doing so well. Just give me a few methods, Jos. Just to stir the juices.

Josie I don't know. You suck me dry of me words, you boys. Use my imagination like a sponge.

Lionel Please, Josie.

Josie Very well. Miss Geraldine. (*She is improvising.*) Your punishment will definitely involve a loofah. Possibly an inappropriately shaped loofah. That has hardened to a crust.

Lionel With barbs on it?

Josie With barbage definitely. My methods will involve said barbed loofah in conjunction with –

Lionel (*growing excitement*) Yes?

Josie Don't rush me. A piece of garden equipment –

Lionel More precise –

Josie A trowel. No. A trowel and fork set. To be used alternately. Front and back.

Lionel Ingenious.

Josie And possibly, in the case of extreme misdemeanour –

Lionel Oh go on –

Josie A trivet. A trivet that is alternately heated up and frozen and then applied to –

Lionel The nipple region?

Josie Certainly somewhere in those environs.

Lionel Hit me with that trivet! Josie, I've got to hand it to you, you're still the best.

Josie You're very kind, but really, Lionel my heart's not in it any more.

Lionel You can still do it though. Sets my pulses racing I can tell you.

Josie I always said that if my body started to crumble, I'd have to pack it in.

Lionel You're still magnificent, Josie. Like a cruise liner.

Josie Well then I should be bloody scuttled. I've an artificial hip looming. I'm on the list. How can I do it with a false hip on the way?

Lionel You're like an opera singer, Josie. You are the Dame Nelly Melba of the domination world. A lashing from you is like an aria, I tell you.

Josie Look at the state of me, Lionel. I'm sick of all the mess. The stains on my carpet.

Lionel Fastest whip in Withington.

Josie Those were the old days, Lionel. Besides, there's only you and Cyril on a Thursday and lately Miss Priscilla's a ball of tension. She wants deluxe service, thigh highs, the works and I can't do it any more, really I can't. And the physical stuff has never been my forte, you know that.

Lionel You're a wordsmith. A poet. You've provided us lads with a service.

Josie Most of the regulars are dead now. Miss Delilah. She was the accountant from Accrington. She went the other week. Sudden it was. Shame. She scrubbed up beautiful dressed as a nun. And Miss Delphine had a triple by-pass not so long back.

Lionel But I'm still up for it.

Josie You only come for the clothes. A bit of dressing up. Anyway, I'm getting rid of all the old cossies.

Lionel Oh no, Jos. You can't. The hours you've spent on them. (*He fingers his dress.*) And they're lovely pieces of work. The fabric alone. They're quality items.

Josie Don't suppose the Sally Army would have much call for them.

Lionel No.

Josie No, I don't suppose. Will you get rid of them for me, Lionel? The rubber won't burn and I don't know what to do with it. I just want shut.

Lionel I don't like hearing you like this. Come on, Jos, it's your birthday.

Josie I'm tired through and through, Lionel.

Lionel I'll put some Elvis on.

Josie No, no, best be quiet. You get yourself changed. Miss Clear'll be here any minute.

Lionel I thought you said it was only me and Priscilla.

Josie No, no, Miss Clear's my cleaner. She does a lovely job too. Obsessive compulsive, you see. Some days I can't get rid of her.

Lionel Could be worse.

Josie She doesn't know about all this. Thinks I'm a therapist.

Lionel Which you are in a way.

Josie She wouldn't like it. She's a raving Catholic. Trust me to land the Pope as my housekeeper. Anyway, that's your lot, pet.

Lionel I don't know how to thank you, Josie.

Josie The usual rates apply, Lionel.

Lionel All taken care of, Josie.

Josie You're a good man, Lionel. And you look quite fetching in a dress. It's a wonder to me that you've never landed yourself a wife.

Lionel Not for the want of trying, Josie. But there you go. It's just one of those things that's passed me by.

He goes to the door.

Josie Lionel, before you leave. I just want to tell you something.

Lionel What is it, Jos?

Josie When I go, Lionel I don't want to be buried.

Lionel What are you saying?

Josie And I don't want to be cremated either. I can't bear heat.

Lionel I don't like this morbid talk, not on your birthday; I won't have it.

Josie I want to be frozen.

Lionel You what?

Josie I read about it. As soon as you die they freeze you. Then they bung you in a casket. With dry ice and stuff.

Lionel Don't talk like this, Josie.

Josie They suspend you. In animation. And then you stay there for hundreds of years in the ice until they wake you up again.

Lionel How do they do that?

Josie They thaw you out and heat you up again.

Lionel How long does that take?

Josie I suppose it depends how much you weigh. Like a turkey.

Lionel You what?

Josie You know, with cooking a turkey, twenty minutes a pound and twenty for luck.

Lionel I prefer chicken.

Josie I've never really got the hang of turkey. One year we ate at half past eleven in the evening. It was in the oven for fourteen hours. Dry as anything it was.

Lionel So once they've defrosted you and heated you up, you'll be alive again?

Josie They'll have to repair me first. All the damage.

Lionel Mmm. Frostbite. Terrible.

Josie And arthritis. They'll have to get rid of me arthritis or there'll be no point.

Lionel I don't know if I'd want to go through it all again. Once is enough.

Josie No. That's what I want. Definitely. Another go at it all.

Lionel Another crack at the whip.

Brenda-Marie hovers in the doorway. She listens to what is said.

Josie Oh no, nothing like that next time. I'm not interested in the body for my next life. I just want my head frozen. I'm not bothered about the rest.

Lionel Just your head?

Josie It's much cheaper anyway, just to have your head done. And next life I want a sit-down job that involves some serious thinking. That'd suit me down to the ground. Anyway, I've worked it all out. I just wanted to say it to someone.

Brenda-Marie enters.

Brenda-Marie Can I be frozen too, Mam? I love the ice, Mam. I'll be the snow queen. I want to be suspended in animation. Like Walt Disney. But I want me whole body, Mam. So that next life I can be International World Ice Dancing Champion. Lionel, I love the ice-dancin' more than football. Me Mam says we're going to get the Sky Television so I can watch the ice-dancin' to the content of me heart. Do you like being one of me Mam's nappy men?

Lionel Yes I do, Brenda-Marie.

Brenda-Marie 'Naughty, naughty boy. Pooed himself all over. Mama's going to smack your bum into next week.' (*She laughs, delighted.*) I'm going to be a domino lady like me Mam.

Josie Dominatrix, love.

Brenda-Marie That's what I said. You've got loads of hair on your legs, Lionel.

Lionel Yes, which is why I must get changed.

Josie That's enough now, love. Calm down. I'll see you out shortly, Lionel.

Lionel exits upstairs

Brenda-Marie If I were 'im, Mam, I wouldn't wear the tights. It doesn't do him any favours.

Josie Lionel likes to wear dresses, love. And you have to wear tights with dresses.

Brenda-Marie It's a shame he can't have some of the hair off his legs on his head, Mam, and then he wouldn't be such a baldy coot.

Josie We're all blessed in different ways, Brenda-Marie.

Brenda-Marie I'm blessed with the ice-dance except I haven't even stepped on the ice, Mam, but sometimes I can feel the ice-dance welling up inside me. The day it comes out will be something special.

Josie That's right, love.

Brenda-Marie I like the nappy men when they wear the maid clothes. And the nurse is not too bad. But when they dress like babbies they look plain stupid, don't they Mam?

Josie Yes, love.

Brenda-Marie I mean like I'm young for me age, aren't I, Mam? But I don't wear the nappies any more.

Josie That's right love.

Brenda-Marie If I was a big man I wouldn't want me Mammy to smack me bum any more.

Josie No. It makes them feel good though, love . . . and it does no harm.

Brenda-Marie I don't think I've got difficulties in the learning like they all say, Mam. It's the meaning of some things I don't understand.

Josie Nor me, love.

Brenda-Marie We've got meaning difficulties, Mam. That's what we've got.

Josie You're right there, love.

Brenda-Marie Mam. I think I might go on holiday.

Josie Oh? Where to this time.

Brenda-Marie I fancy Zanzibar.

Josie Exotic.

Brenda-Marie Can you go skiing there, Mam?

Josie I'm not sure. I think it's more of a hot and spicy place.

Brenda-Marie (*disappointed*) Oh. I'll have to stay 'ere then.

Josie Never mind, eh? I'm tired now, Brenda-Marie.

Brenda-Marie My Mammy needs her rest.

Lionel re-enters in a suit.

Brenda-Marie Your legs look heaps better in them slacks, Lionel.

Lionel Thank you, Brenda-Marie. Now what would you say to a party this evening for your Mam's birthday?

Brenda-Marie Oh yes! We never have parties.

Josie No, no Lionel. I don't want a party. I'm too old.

Brenda-Marie We've never had a party since our Shelly-Louise went on up to heaven.

Josie No, it's a ridiculous idea. We've got no friends. And I'm too tired.

Lionel Too late. It's arranged. I'm coming and Brenda-Marie is coming and I'm going to invite someone else.

Josie Who?

Lionel It's a surprise.

Brenda-Marie I love it when someone's coming.

Josie Not Miss Priscilla.

Lionel Not her. Someone much more exciting.

Brenda-Marie Someone hardly ever comes here. Except the nappy men and we don't count them.

Josie No, no, Lionel, really I don't want a party.

Lionel It's too late. Get your glad rags on. I'll bring some bottles. I'll be back here around seven.

Brenda-Marie It's like advent. That's my favourite time of the year. With the calendar.

Josie I've got no food for a party.

Lionel A bit of tinned ham will do. You must have that.

Josie No, no, you can't have tinned ham any more. You have to have those other things. Crustini. They sell them in Marks.

Lionel We don't need food.

Brenda-Marie Opening all the doors on the calendar. Waiting for the really important person to come.

Josie I'm really not bothered, Lionel.

Lionel You're sixty today, Josie. We must celebrate. Now go and have a lie-down. And I'll see you later.

Martha enters with shopping.

Martha One, two, three, four, five . . . I'm sorry, Mrs Botting. I got overwhelmed by the numbers on my bus ticket so I only managed the local shop.

Brenda-Marie Holy Jo's got this thing about numbers, Lionel.

Martha I managed to get the milk but I didn't trust the cheese.

Josie That's fine, Miss Clear. This is Mr Lionel Trills. Miss Martha Clear.

Lionel Enchanted, Miss Clear. (*He holds out his hand to her.*)

Martha One, two, three, four, five. I'm afraid I don't shake hands, Mr Trills.

Lionel Ah. No, no, of course not.

Martha Not that I'm implying that your hands are contaminated in some way.

Lionel I hope not.

Martha Although people these days barely wash their hands, you know. It used to be standard but is sadly dying out.

Brenda-Marie My Mam makes me wash mine after I've done a wee.

Josie Yes, all right, Brenda-Marie.

Lionel How often would you think was acceptable, Miss Clear?

Martha Well, I wash mine thirty-five times a day. But I tend to do most things in multiples of five.

Lionel Really? I wouldn't say that I washed mine that many times. But being a dry cleaner I would say that I washed mine more than the average.

Martha That's very refreshing to hear, Mr Trills.

Lionel I use a lot of hand cream too. The chemicals involved in dry cleaning do dry my skin.

Martha I'm not sure where I stand on hand cream, Mr Trills. It's not something I use as a rule.

Lionel No.

Martha But being a dry cleaner must be a very rewarding profession.

Lionel It has its moments.

Martha I can imagine. Taking all that soiled laundry and turning it into something fresh and clean. Yes.

Josie Have you got some change for me, Miss Clear?

Martha Oh yes. I beg your pardon, Mrs Botting. One, two, three, four, five –

Josie Come on now, Bren, we've got lots to do to get ready.

Lionel Ah yes, Miss Clear. We're having a party this evening to celebrate Josie's birthday. Perhaps you'd like to come.

Martha (*flustered*) Oh no, no, no thank you. One, two, three, four, five.

Josie Oh I don't know, Lionel. We don't want to make this into an event.

Lionel But it is an event, Josie.

Martha I haven't been invited to a party since I came to England.

Lionel When was that?

Martha 1971.

Lionel Well I feel it's rather essential that you join us this evening.

Martha Oh no. I don't go out normally after the hour that follows five.

Brenda-Marie You mean six o'clock?

Josie Brenda-Marie.

Lionel You surprise me, Miss Clear. I had you marked down as a party animal.

Martha Oh no, no, no, Mr Trills. My sister Mary was the raver. I was always a home-bird.

Lionel But I hope for Josie's sake that tonight will prove the exception to the rule.

Brenda-Marie Someone else is coming who's special but we don't know who it is, Holy Jo.

Lionel Well that's settled then.

Brenda-Marie I'm going to get ready. Mam, will you help me get ready?

Josie Come on then. I'll take that, Miss Clear.

She takes the groceries.

Lionel I'll see myself out, Josie.

Brenda-Marie and Josie exit.

SCENE THREE

As before.

Martha I must be on my way too.

Lionel Can I drop you off anywhere, Miss Clear?

Martha Oh no I don't think so.

Lionel Really it's no trouble.

Martha What sort of car do you have?

Lionel A Nissan Micra. It's very reliable.

Martha No, I mean the colour and numberplate.

Lionel It's green. s559 JOY. Does it make a difference?

Martha No, that sounds all right to me. Joy.

Lionel What?

Martha You have joy in your numberplate.

Lionel Yes, I suppose I do.

Martha Mr Trills do you ever have the overwhelming sensation that you may have hit someone in the road without realising it?

Lionel No I can't say that I do.

Martha That you might for instance have inadvertently caused a large motorway pile-up by for example braking very suddenly and leaving sharply by an exit road without indicating?

Lionel No, I have to say I've never felt like that.

Martha I've never driven myself, you see, but I thought that might be the case.

Lionel Not usually, I don't think . . . So where would you like to go?

Martha No, no, Mr Trills. Thank you all the same I'd like to walk. One, two, three, four, five.

Lionel As you wish, Miss Clear. But I will see you later?

Martha I don't really, one, two, three, no, I don't really go to, four, five, parties.

Lionel Nor do I, to tell the honest truth.

Martha Even in Ireland I didn't.

Lionel I never had a party when I was small. Never once.

Martha I went to a lot of wakes. But that's not really the same.

Lionel My Mother didn't like people rucking up the carpet. 'Son, I'm not one for mayhem,' she used to say.

Martha I can see her point.

Lionel It made me yearn for mayhem though, don't you see? . . . I think you have to be taught how to party from a tender age. I think there's an art to it.

Martha I wouldn't know.

Lionel So tonight we will both be virgins. We can slowly let our hair down together.

Martha That won't take very long in your case, Mr Trills.

Lionel Alas no. Whereas in yours it may take all night. Your hair really is very long, Miss Clear.

Martha Thank you.

Lionel It must take an age to wash.

Martha It does.

Lionel I really don't think I could cope.

Martha It's the drying that's really wearing. A normal hairdrier just doesn't have the stamina with my hair.

Lionel Do you know what you could do? Pop it in a trouser press.

Martha That really doesn't appeal, Mr Trills.

Lionel No. It must be a long time since you had it cut.

Martha We don't cut our hair in my family till we are married. It's tradition.

Lionel I've never heard of that before.

Martha Hairdressers are the least trustworthy of people, Mr Trills. They rank below robbers in my opinion.

Lionel Really?

Martha Yes, well, one, two, three, four, five. I really must be on my way, Mr Trills. I can't spend my day in idle chatter with strange men. Particularly strange men with a hair fixation.

Lionel Oh forgive me, Miss Clear, I didn't mean to offend you. Your hair is truly remarkable.

Martha And yours is truly absent. Now if you don't mind.

Lionel I don't mind. There were a few years when I did. When I used to hang upside down from doors and the like. To encourage growth.

Martha I beg your pardon?

Lionel To stimulate the follicles.

Martha I really don't wish to know.

Lionel But now I've grown to rather like it.

Martha Good for you.

Lionel It's a funny thing but you can always tell how I'm feeling from my head. If I'm particularly chipper my pate gets a lovely sheen to it. Like a polished apple. A Worcester Pearmain or a Russet Gold. But if I'm feeling under the weather, it looks grey, my head. Positively grey. What colour would you say it was now?

He lowers his head in her direction.

Martha I really have no interest in the shine or otherwise of your head, Mr Trills.

Lionel I should think it's a fairly good colour today. Not quite a Granny Smith but a definite Golden Delicious.

Martha I would advise you to invest in a hat, Mr Trills. All the men in my family wore hats. Very little can go awry when you're sporting a nice trilby. That's what my Father used to say.

Lionel Oh no, Miss Clear I like to air my head. Let the oxygen get to my brain.

Martha One, two, three, four, five. Yes, well, as I say, Mr Trills I'm in rather a hurry.

Lionel Do you find bald men unattractive, Miss Clear?

Martha Really, Mr Trills, I'm amazed by your, one, two, three, four, five – but since you ask I've always preferred a full head of hair in a man. Now Elvis had beautiful hair. Thick and black. And I do have a soft spot for a quiff. Oh yes, an Elvis quiff can be guaranteed to wet my whistle so to speak.

Lionel (*sadly*) I see.

Martha I didn't mean to offend, Mr Trills. I'm sure there are women who favour men who are – challenged in the hair department, such as yourself.

Lionel No I don't think so, Miss Clear. I think I can say from experience that a woman prefers to have something to run her fingers through.

Martha But I could imagine a situation where a lady might get equal pleasure from say, taking a duster and some Mr Sheen and giving your head a good old buff and polish.

Lionel I wish that I had encountered such a lady, Miss Clear, I really do.

Martha Perhaps you could grow a beard.

Lionel No, Miss Clear, forgive me but I think few women are fooled by a bald man with a beard. It is almost impossible to compensate for the loss of head hair. And trying to divert a lady's attention to full chin growth seldom makes a good impression.

Martha No, I suppose not. Well we all have our crosses to bear.

Lionel Indeed.

Martha After you, Mr Trills.

She gestures towards the door.

Lionel No, after you, Miss Clear.

Martha No please.

Lionel No I insist.

Martha Mr Trills it is absolutely essential that you leave before I do. Believe me.

Lionel I'm not about to run off with the house silver, Miss Clear.

Martha Goodbye, Mr Trills. Really I'm growing very tired of your company and if I am to come to this party this evening it would be better if you didn't overstay your welcome right now.

Lionel Enough said, Miss Clear. I do admire a woman who doesn't mince her words.

Martha My words are never minced, Mr Trills.

Lionel No indeed, your words are tenderized with a large hammer. Well. It's been a pleasure. I look forward to seeing you later. In your glad rags, mind.

Martha Goodbye, Mr Trills.

He exits.

Glad rags. I'd catch my death. (*She shuts the door rapidly behind him. She raps the door and turns the doorknob rapidly.*) One, two, three, four, five. One, two, three, four, five. One, two three, four, five. (*She exits through the door. We hear her repeat the procedure on the other side of the door as lights fade.*) One, two, three, four, five. One, two, three, four, five. One two, three, four, five.

SCENE FOUR

Music: Elvis Presley, 'Party'.

  Josie enters. She has changed, but she hasn't made a big effort with her appearance. She brings various party food and arranges it. She sings absently along to the record. She opens a packet of nuts that sprays all over the floor. She begins to cry. As she is crying, Brenda-Marie enters. Brenda-Marie is wearing an improbable party dress and heavy make-up.

Brenda-Marie Don't do the crying, Mam. You know I hate the crying.

Josie I'm not crying, Bren love. Switch that record off for me.

Brenda-Marie They're only peanuts, Mam. You shouldn't cry over spilt peanuts.

Josie I think it's me tear ducts. I think they must be infected. I go out into the wind and my eyes pour. But then it's a cold wind at the moment.

Brenda-Marie It's going to snow, Mam. Any day. Maybe tonight.

Josie Let's get these nuts picked up. I don't know, having a party at my age.

Brenda-Marie You're still young, Mammy.

Josie What would I do without you, Brenda-Marie?

Brenda-Marie You'd be lost, Mam.

Josie You're right there, love.

Brenda-Marie I have to fill up the space for two in your heart.

Josie What do you mean?

Brenda-Marie When we lost our Shelly-Louise . . .
I bought you a happy birthday present.

Josie You don't have to go spending your money on me.

Brenda-Marie It was dirt cheap.

She hands her a crudely wrapped package.

Josie Thank you, love.

Josie opens the present. Inside is a snowscene.

Brenda-Marie If you don't want it, I'll have it.

Josie No. No. I love it.

Brenda-Marie You can shake it, Mam and the snow
falls. See that's like our house. And I'm like that girl
outside, dancing in the snow. Shake it again, Mam.
Make it snow again. Shall I keep it in my room for safe-keeping?

Josie What a good idea, love.

Brenda-Marie And then if I'm away for a short while
and you're missing me, you can shake it and see me
dance in the snow.

Josie Where are you going?

Brenda-Marie Haven't decided yet, Mam. I'll send you a
postcard.

Josie Yes or I'll worry.

Brenda-Marie I might go to Acapulco. I've always fancied that.

Josie Lovely.

Brenda-Marie Or I might not bother. I might just stay here.

Josie Whatever suits you, Brenda-Marie.

The doorbell goes. It is the first few bars of 'The Wonder of You'.

Josie There's the front door.

Brenda-Marie I wonder if it's the special person.

Josie It's probably Lionel.

She goes to the front door. Brenda-Marie shakes the snowscene.

Brenda-Marie And here we are on holiday on ice. Brenda-Marie Botting is doing the dance of the ice queen. Look at her go. She's brilliant.

Martha enters. She's looking very dressed up, in a rather bizarre crochet dress. Her hair is done very elaborately. She quickly does her door routine – just the doorknob this time and she counts silently. She calls back to Josie.

Martha I can't seem to shake that man, Mrs Botting. He's following me up the drive there. I think he may have the tendency to be a stalker.

Josie Lionel? I better let him in.

She exits again.

Martha He seems to be struggling with rather a large box of alcoholic beverages. I think he's intent on getting us all intoxicated.

Brenda-Marie Holy Jo! You look like Mortitia.

Martha I assume this is not a favourable comparison.

Brenda-Marie We didn't think you'd come. Me and me Mam.

Martha No, well I was in two minds myself. More than two minds. (*She spreads out a small scarf on the sofa and sits on it.*)

Brenda-Marie Were you in five minds, Holy Jo?

Martha I'm not going to rise to you this evening. I'm barely conscious of you. If I feel the urge to count, I shall do so silently. Counting like prayer can be silent.

Brenda-Marie Your dress is full of holes.

Josie re-enters.

Josie It's a lovely dress, Miss Clear.

Martha Thank you, I made it myself.

Brenda-Marie You left loads of bits out.

Josie I never mastered crochet myself.

Brenda-Marie It could be a table-cloth.

Martha I used to be a big fan of needlepoint. But most patterns are by numbers, so –

Josie Of course.

Brenda-Marie Where's Lionel?

Josie He's in the kitchen putting some of the bottles in the fridge. Why don't you offer Miss Clear a crisp, Brenda-Marie?

Brenda-Marie slouches over to the table and takes the crisps.

Martha Thank you very much, Brenda-Marie. (*She takes a wet one from her bag, hastily wipes her hands, then takes some crisps.*)

Brenda-Marie Do you know how many crisps you've got there, Holy Jo? I'd say about – six.

Josie That's enough, Brenda.

Martha throws the crisps back, visibly stiffens, counts silently to herself, resumes in her normal voice.

Martha You know Mrs Botting, I read a most disturbing report the other day. About Bombay Mix.

Josie Did you really?

Brenda-Marie What's that?

Josie It's what you get in Indian restaurants isn't it? Like Indian crisps.

Martha That's right. Apparently they examined some of this Bombay Mix under the microscope and found five different types of men's urine in it.

Brenda-Marie How many different types of men's urine are there?

Josie I don't know, love.

Martha It was the urine of five different men, I believe. Not different types of urine. Although I am not an expert on men's urine.

Brenda-Marie Five different men weed in the Bombay Mix? Didn't anybody notice?

Martha They didn't urinate in the mix. They went to the bathroom, failed to wash themselves after doing their business, then plunged their hands into the bowl when it was proffered to them.

Josie I don't know what the world's coming to.

Martha That's why I steer clear of restaurants.

Brenda-Marie Do you want a nut, Holy Jo?

Martha Thank you. (*She takes a nut, puts it to her mouth, hesitates.*)

Josie You're all right, Miss Clear. I haven't had five different types of men round here today.

Brenda-Marie We've had all sorts of men come round here though, haven't we, Mam?

Martha (*startled*) What?

Josie She means – door-to-door salesmen. At one time we had a spate of door-to-door salemen. You know, encyclopedias. Plagued, we were.

Martha I will have no truck with hawkers myself.

Josie No, nor me, Miss Clear.

Martha smiles and pops the nut in her mouth.

Brenda-Marie You dropped them nuts on the floor earlier, didn't you, Mam?

Martha nearly chokes. Josie goes to her aid. Lionel enters with a hostess trolley of drinks.

Josie Yes, but my floor's good enough to eat off, thanks to you, Miss Clear.

Martha I'm all right. Please don't fuss.

Lionel Here we are then. Drinks all round. I think you're in desperate need of lubrication, Miss Clear.

Martha Water please.

Lionel Water to start with. But I've got a treat for you ladies. I've made my special cocktail. It's called a catastrophe.

Brenda-Marie I want a catastrophe!

Lionel And you shall have one, my sweet. One for Josie first, our birthday queen.

Josie Thank you, Lionel. Ooh, that'd put some hairs on your chest.

Brenda-Marie You need a drink that puts them on your head, Lionel.

Lionel Still working on that recipe. There we go, Brenda-Marie.

Josie Don't drink it all down in one. Your head'll be spinning.

Lionel Can I tempt you, Miss Clear?

Martha No, thank you, I'm fine with the water.

Brenda-Marie When's the special person coming, Lionel?

Lionel Any minute.

Josie I hope it's a nice surprise. I'm not up for any big shocks.

Lionel You'll love it. You look very lovely this evening, if you don't mind my saying, Miss Clear.

Martha Don't get fresh with me, Mr Trills. I know your sort of old.

Josie Miss Clear. Lionel paid you a compliment.

Martha Yes, I've had men pay me compliments before and I know where it leads.

Brenda-Marie What did they pay you compliments about, Holy Jo?

Martha I was very sought after when I was young.

Lionel I've no doubt.

Martha But men just want one thing.

Brenda-Marie What's that?

Martha They want you to clean up after them.

Josie It's true. There's always a lot more laundry where men are concerned.

Martha Unspeakable stains.

Brenda-Marie But you like that, Holy Jo. Your favourite thing is getting rid of unspeakable stains.

Josie But our Lionel isn't like that. He's very clean and tidy. The only thing he might want to get his hands on are your dresses.

Martha What?

Lionel (*quickly*) It sounds to me like you've had your fingers burnt where men are concerned, Miss Clear.

Martha A lot more than my fingers I can tell you.

Josie Were you married once, Miss Clear?

Martha No it never got to that. It was all very short-lived. The summer of 'sixty-nine.

Josie A holiday romance?

Martha Funeral.

Josie What?

Martha More of a funeral romance. I met him at my Uncle Padraic's wake.

Lionel Perhaps not the most romantic of settings.

Martha I thought he had the look of Gene Pitney about him or I wouldn't have bothered.

Josie They were all after looking like him or Elvis those days.

Martha I should never have gone for a Gene Pitney. Even one of the Everly Brothers would have been better.

Lionel It's only twenty-four hours from Tulsa.

Martha If only that were true, Mr Trills.

Lionel Gene Pitney was small wasn't he?

Josie Oh yes. He was a dwarf.

Brenda-Marie What did Gene Pitney do to you, Holy Jo?

Martha He did unmentionables, Brenda-Marie.

Brenda-Marie Go on.

Martha Don't press me on this now, Brenda-Marie.

Brenda-Marie Go on, tell me, Holy Jo. What did he do?

Lionel He stepped on her blue-suede shoes.

Brenda-Marie giggles.

Martha This is a difficult memory for me, Mr Trills, I'd appreciate a little respect.

Lionel I'm sorry Miss Clear.

Martha Suffice to say, Mrs Botting, he did the dirty on me. With an altar boy from Our Lady of Pity. I should have known. He had skulduggery written all over his face.

Brenda-Marie That must have looked funny.

Josie It must have been very hard for you, Miss Clear.

Martha It's one of the main reasons I came over here, Mrs Botting. To escape the skuldugger. Since that escapade I've given men very short shrift, I don't mind telling you.

Lionel But we're not all skulduggers, Miss Clear.

Martha No. But I've come to terms with it, Mr Trills. Some women are not born to be brides. It must be genetic.

Josie You're right there, Miss Clear.

Martha Spinster is such a lonely word though, don't you think, Mrs Botting?

Lionel It's no worse than bachelor.

Martha (*with feeling*) Oh yes, it's much worse, Mr Trills. Much, much worse. But you were blessed Mrs Botting. I never hear you mention Mr Botting. Has he passed on?

Josie Passed out more like. Suffice to say, I wasn't blessed for very long, Miss Clear.

Martha But long enough to have a beautiful daughter.

Brenda-Marie I'll never be a bride.

Lionel Of course you will, Brenda-Marie.

Brenda-Marie All I want is to be a bride for a day and for everyone to throw confetti at me because that's like love and money and stars all over you all at once. But no-one will ever throw confetti at me.

Lionel Of course they will.

Brenda-Marie No, I've been left on the ledge.

Josie On the shelf, I think you mean, love.

Brenda-Marie No, it's too narrow for a shelf. It's definitely a ledge.

Josie Some young man will snap you up, love.

Brenda-Marie No, Shelly-Louise was the one they would have snapped up. No-one will marry me. I'm too simple.

Lionel Ah but simplicity in a woman is much sought after, Brenda-Marie. I'm often asked what are the top three qualities you look for in a woman and I say, 'Good looks, sweet breath and gentle simplicity' every time. And you have those three qualities in abundance, Brenda-Marie.

Brenda-Marie Yeah but I'm not marrying you, Lionel. You're far too old for me. And I could never marry one of the nappy men.

Martha The who?

Lionel Happy men.

Josie (*overlapping with Lionel*) Clappy men.

Pause.

Lionel You know, happy-clappy men.

Josie It's one of her peculiar turns of phrase, Miss Clear. Your prince will come one day, Brenda-Marie.

Lionel Another catastrophe, Josie?

Josie I don't mind if I do.

Brenda-Marie I want a coca-cola. With lots of ice.

Lionel Coming up. Miss Clear?

Martha I think I'd like half a catastrophe. Just to try.

Josie Don't go mad now, Miss Clear.

The doorbell rings: it is the first few bars of 'Are You Lonesome Tonight?'

Lionel And there's the bell! Aha! Our mystery guest has arrived. Are you ready for this now, ladies?

Brenda-Marie Hurray! The surprise person is here.

Josie I don't know if I'm going to enjoy this.

Lionel Sit tight, now ladies. I'll go. You could maybe dim the lights for a bit of ambience.

Lionel exits to the front door. The women prepare the room.

Martha I very much hope this is going to be legal.

Brenda-Marie I don't.

Josie I don't think I can bear any excitement.

Martha I hope it's not a brass band. I can't abide brass bands.

Josie What on earth made you think it would be a brass band, Miss Clear?

Martha Brass bands pop up at the most inopportune moments in my experience.

Brenda-Marie A brass band wouldn't fit in here.

Martha My Father played the cornet. Until someone put him out of his misery.

Josie I don't care who it is, so long as they're quiet.

Brenda-Marie It might be Father Christmas. He always comes at the end of Advent.

Josie No, he's only just been, love.

Brenda-Marie (*sadly*) Oh yeah.

Martha It's probably just a fellow dry-cleaner.

Josie Lionel works on his own; runs his own business.

Martha But he probably moves in dry-cleaning circles.

Josie I don't think they necessarily stick together, Miss Clear. Dry cleaners are not primarily known for their pack instinct.

Martha People with an interest in cleanliness have to stick together these days, Mrs Botting. We're a dying breed.

Lionel re-enters. He is brimming with excitement.

Lionel Are we all set then, ladies?

Brenda-Marie Holy Jo thinks it's going to be a brass band. But I think it might be Father Christmas calling round early like.

Lionel Wrong and wrong again.

Josie So long as it's not the vice squad, we'll be all right.

Martha Why would it be the vice squad, Mrs Botting?

Josie A figure of speech, Miss Clear. Come on then, Lionel. The suspense is killing us.

Lionel He's ready for you.

Martha So it is a he.

Brenda-Marie I think I might faint when the surprise man comes in.

Lionel No you won't now, Brenda-Marie.

Josie Take a deep breath, Brenda-Marie. No man is worth fainting over.

Lionel Hold on to your seats then, ladies, I give you our special mystery guest.

He goes to the door and does the thumbs-up.

Ready when you are, Mr Wong.

*The Chinese Elvis enters. He is a young Vietnamese man
who is fully kitted as a young (Jailhouse Rock-type)
Elvis. He launches into his act with gusto – Elvis hip
thrusts and gyrations and curling lip – but it's obvious
that he's nervous. He brings a small tape recorder for
his backing music – perhaps he plugs a microphone into
it. When he speaks he has a strong Manchester accent.
The Chinese Elvis gives Lionel a signal to switch on his
music.*

Chinese Elvis
    Well since my baby left me
    I've found a new place to dwell
    Down at the end of lonely street
    At Heartbreak Hotel,
    I'm so lonely, baby
    I'm so lonely
    I'm so lonely
    That I could die.

Good evening, ladies and gentleman. My name is
Timothy Wong and I will be your Elvis for the evening . . .
(*He clears his throat to make his presentation, which
is rather bad.*) His name was Elvis Aaron Presley. His
records have sold over one billion copies around the
world. He made thirty-three hit movies. He became one
of the highest paid performers in the history of Las
Vegas. His name was Elvis Aaron Presley. His is the story
of a raw talent and humble beginnings rising to huge
success and an unbelievable stage charisma. His name
was Elvis Aaron Presley.

Martha We know what his name was.

Lionel Carry on, lad. You're doing grand.

Chinese Elvis I've lost my place now . . . Um . . . Elvis Aaron Presley. Umm. Sorry about this.

Josie Just cut to the chase, lad.

Chinese Elvis Okay. Tonight I bring you a taste of that Elvis magic into your front room. Where two or three people are gathered in the name of Elvis, his magic can live on.

Martha Oh yes, I like that.

Chinese Elvis Yes Madam, Elvis lives on through me and people like me. Think of your requests now. I will undertake any of the King's hits. The thin years or the fat years. Because this night is for you and you alone. A private audience with the King of Rock and Roll.

> Now if your baby leaves you
> And you gotta tale to tell
> Just take a walk down lonely street
> To Heartbreak Hotel, where you'll be
> You'll be so lonely, baby
> And I'll be lonely,
> We'll be so lonely
> That we could die.

Thank you very much. (*à la Elvis*)

> *A pause.*
> *Lionel and Brenda-Marie clap ferociously. Martha and Josie look sceptical.*

Lionel Fantastic! That was great!

Brenda-Marie Elvis is alive!

Josie Well. He doesn't look much like him, does he?

Brenda-Marie And he's a Chinaman!

Josie And I don't know if he sounds much like him either.

Lionel Josie!

Martha I don't know if I hold with these Elvis impersonators.

Josie No, nor do I.

Martha They get everywhere. At the end of the day, there's nothing like the real thing.

Josie No.

Lionel Ladies, please, a bit of respect for Elvis.

Brenda-Marie I like him.

Chinese Elvis Do you think I could use your toilet? I'm busting. It must have been all that standing about in the cold.

Josie Go ahead.

Lionel Here we go, Tim, I'll show you the way.

Chinese Elvis Give you a minute to think of your requests.

Lionel exits with the Chinese Elvis.

Josie I read about a Chinese Elvis the other day who was up for aggravated bodily harm.

Martha No!

Josie He worked in a Chinese Elvis restaurant and he used to duff up the customers. If they didn't like the food. Which was atrocious by all accounts.

Martha No!

Josie Yes!

Brenda-Marie He went prawn crackers. (*She laughs delightedly.*)

Martha You don't think it could be the same one?

Josie I hope not. I think he was older. But I read about another Chinese Elvis who used his position to lure young women into bed.

Martha That's sacrilege that is. I'm going right off him.

Josie They can be a funny lot.

Lionel re-enters.

Lionel Josie, what are you like? You ought to give the poor kid some encouragement. He's in tatters up there, you know.

Martha Has he ever been involved in a fracas?

Lionel What?

Martha You know. He's never caused a public affray?

Lionel No. Not as far as I know.

Martha No kind of kerfuffle whatsoever?

Lionel No, what do you mean?

Josie You read terrible things. Lionel. In the papers. About Chinese Elvis impersonators. We were just checking.

Lionel I thought it would be a nice surprise.

Josie How do you know him?

Lionel He's from that Kissagram company round the corner from me. I dry-clean all their outfits. They've got a few Elvises.

Brenda-Marie Are they all Chinese?

Lionel What?

Martha Oh no. I bet not. Elvis comes in all shapes and sizes these days. You get all sorts trying it. Norwegian, African, I even heard that you can get an Eskimo Elvis.

Brenda-Marie Oh yes! An Elvis that lives in an igloo.

Josie They're all at it.

Martha They have conventions.

Josie I bet they do.

Martha They sky-dive out of aeroplanes. I think it's an insult.

Josie It makes a mockery of the King.

Brenda-Marie I think it would be lovely. Lots of Elvis's falling out of the sky. Like snow.

Martha They're just trying to muscle in on the act. Capture some of his reflected glory.

Lionel Well I'm very sorry, ladies. I'm sorry to disappoint you. I thought you'd enjoy it, Josie. Really I did.

Josie Oh yes, yes, Lionel. It was a lovely surprise.

Lionel I can ask him to go now.

Martha No. Not now he's made the effort.

Lionel I mean, I thought you loved Elvis. And when you looked a bit glum today, I thought this would be the perfect pick-me-up.

Josie Oh I do love Elvis. Elvis has helped me get through many a dark hour, I can tell you.

Martha Me too.

Josie I didn't know you were partial, Miss Clear.

Martha Everyone's partial to Elvis.

Brenda-Marie That's what Mam says. Even if you don't like Elvis, you like Elvis don't you, Mam?

Josie That's right.

Martha I'd go as far as to say that Elvis has been the saving grace of my life, Mrs Botting. There's been times when circumstance has laid me low, but just a few bars of 'A Big Hunk of Love' and I come bouncing back.

Josie I know what you're saying, Miss Clear. Elvis has always been there for me too. Especially when I lost our Shelly-Louise.

Martha Mrs Botting, as a Catholic I pray for the Second Coming but, do you know, what I hope and God forgive me for saying this, Mrs Botting, I hope when He comes again that He'll be wearing rhinestones and singing 'Love Me Tender'.

Josie That's a beautiful image you've summoned for us, Miss Clear.

Martha Call me Martha, Mrs Botting.

Josie He's a long time in that lavatory, Lionel. What's he doing?

Lionel I don't know.

Martha I hope whatever he's doing that he washes his hands afterwards.

Lionel Well, you were a bit harsh on him. He's a nervous type, Josie. I really think he felt a bit crushed earlier. He might have lost his bottle. Apparently he's only just starting out as an Elvis. If you want him to stay you'll have to be a bit more encouraging to the lad.

Josie I didn't mean to be discouraging. He's got a nice voice. It took me by surprise, that's all. I hope he's all right.

Martha I hope there hasn't been some sort of tragic accident. We all know how Elvis died, God rest his soul.

I hope this Chinese fellow wasn't so disheartened by our lack of enthusiasm that he has decided to end it all in a bizarre Elvis copy-cat suicide.

Brenda-Marie How did Elvis die?

Josie On the toilet, love. You do have a tendency to look on the black side, Miss Clear.

Martha Stranger things have happened, Mrs Botting. It could be a pact. All the Elvis impersonators in the world deciding to end it all. In true Elvis style.

Josie And the Chinese are all for a bit of hara-kiri.

Lionel That's the Japanese.

Josie You'd better check on him all the same, Lionel. You might have to coax him down.

Brenda-Marie No, he's coming! The Chinese Elvis is still alive!

Chinese Elvis re-enters.

Josie Ah you had us all worried there, love.

Chinese Elvis Sorry. I got caught short.

Lionel This is the birthday girl, Tim. This is Josie.

Josie Elvis. You must call him Elvis. I'm sorry we weren't more encouraging before, Elvis.

Chinese Elvis That's okay. I'm a bit of a beginner to tell the truth.

Josie But there's a lot of potential there, I can tell you. You've the makings of a real Elvis.

Chinese Elvis Do you think so?

Martha Oh yes, and we don't hold with Elvis impersonators as a rule.

Brenda-Marie I'd like to see you fall like snow, Chinese Elvis.

Josie He hasn't got time for that now Brenda-Marie. Well, is it request time?

Chinese Elvis Oh yes, Josie. What can I sing for you? For your birthday.

Josie Let's see now.

Brenda-Marie Marie's the name of his latest flame! Let's have that. Only you can sing, Brenda-Marie's the name of his latest flame, if you want, Elvis.

Chinese Elvis I don't do that one.

Martha What about 'Love Me Tender'? That's my favourite.

Chinese Elvis I haven't learned that one yet either.

Martha But I thought you said you could do the full complement.

Lionel He's only just getting going. Give the lad a chance.

Chinese Elvis I haven't got that many under my belt yet.

Martha Well what can you do?

Josie I know what I'd like.

She whispers in the Chinese Elvis's ear.

Josie Can you do that one?

Chinese Elvis I'll have a go. I'm a bit ropy on the second verse.

Lionel We'll help you out, lad.

Chinese Elvis Ladies and Lionel. Here's a little song that's going out to our birthday girl, this evening. This is from Elvis to Josie to say 'Happy Birthday'.

Martha An Elvis impersonator who doesn't know any of the songs, I don't know.

Brenda-Marie Shush, Holy Jo.

Chinese Elvis
Maybe I didn't treat you
Quite as good as I should have

Lionel (*over the singing*) Lovely choice, Josie.

Josie I'll have another catastrophe now, thank you Lionel.

Brenda-Marie Uh oh. This is me Mam's mascara down the face song.

Chinese Elvis
Maybe I didn't love you
Quite as often as I could have
Little things I should have said and done
I just never took the time
You were always on my mind
You were always –

The front door bell goes. The Chinese Elvis pauses his tape deck.

Josie Who's that? We're not expecting anyone else are we, Lionel?

Lionel No.

Brenda-Marie It's another mystery guest. Shall I go?

Martha Perhaps it's another Elvis. Perhaps we're to be thronged with Elvises this evening.

Lionel Elvii, isn't it, if there's more than one?

Josie You go if you want, Brenda-Marie love. It's probably kids messing about.

Chinese Elvis Shall I carry on?

Josie Yes, Elvis, if you would. I was loving every minute of that.

Chinese Elvis
Maybe I didn't hold you
All those lonely lonely times
And I guess I never told you
I'm so happy that you're mine
If I made you feel second best
Girl I'm so sorry I was blind
You were always on my mind
You were always on my mind.

During the last three lines, Brenda-Marie re-enters, followed by Louise. Josie and Louise stare at each other. It is as if everyone is suspended in time for a minute except the Chinese Elvis who continues to sing. The words overlap with the music.

Chinese Elvis
Tell me, tell me that your sweet love hasn't died –

Brenda-Marie I don't know who it is. But I think it might be Audrey Hepburn.

Josie Oh God!

Lionel What is it, Josie?

Chinese Elvis
Give me, give me one more chance
To keep you satisfied, satisfied.

Brenda-Marie She said you'd want to see her.

Martha Are you all right there, Mrs Botting?

Brenda-Marie (*suddenly with awe. She walks around her sister.*) I know who you are. I know what happened to you. They froze you, didn't they? Then they thawed you

60

out. And warmed you up. And now you're alive again! You're alive!

From now on the characters speak after each sung line.

Chinese Elvis
Little things I should have said and done

Brenda-Marie Is it her, Mam?

Chinese Elvis
I just never took the time

Brenda-Marie (*euphoric*) It's her, isn't it Mam?

Chinese Elvis
You were always on my mind

Lionel Josie?

Chinese Elvis
You were always on my mind

Louise Mother?

Josie (*her voice is almost a gasp*) Shelly-Louise?

Louise Happy birthday, Mother.

Martha Holy Mary, Mother of God! It's a miracle.

Chinese Elvis
You were always on my mind

Pause

Chinese Elvis (*à la Elvis*) Thank you very much.

Blackout. Original Elvis version of 'Always on My Mind' takes over.
  End of Act One.

Act Two

SCENE ONE

Incidental music: Elvis Presley, 'It's Now or Never'.
    Louise looks out of the window. Perhaps she blows on the window and starts to write HELP as the Chinese Elvis enters. He wears an Elvis GI costume. He doesn't see Louise at first. She watches him.

Louise Boo!

Chinese Elvis (*jumps*) Oh! Sorry.

Louise What's the matter? Look like you've seen a ghost.

Chinese Elvis No, I didn't realise you were –

Louise Nice costume. Sexy. Now who do you remind me of in that?

Chinese Elvis Well, I'm supposed to be –

Louise It was a joke, Elvis!

Chinese Elvis Oh. Right. I like to change a couple of times in my act. Give people their money's worth. Especially cause I'm not on top of all the songs yet.

Louise Style over content. Much more important.

    Pause. He doesn't know how to take her.

Chinese Elvis Where is everybody?

Louise Brenda-Marie's in her tent. She won't come out apparently. I don't know about the others. I think I've scared them all off.

Chinese Elvis Oh, right.

    Pause

62

Louise So what's it like being an Elvis impersonator?

Chinese Elvis It's better than working in a restaurant.

Louise I'm not that mad on Elvis. I mean, he took loads of drugs, he ate too much and he married Priscilla when she was about twelve.

Chinese Elvis Right, yeah. Sorry.

Louise No, don't apologise. It's not your fault.

Chinese Elvis Well, I suppose I'll go and find Lionel.

Louise No, don't go. It's nice to have some company. Sorry, I haven't introduced myself. I'm the dead daughter. I'm Shelly-Louise.

Chinese Elvis Pleased to meet you.

Louise Except I've changed my name to Louise. I felt I couldn't grow old with a name like Shelly-Louise.

Chinese Elvis I see.

Pause

Louise Oh! And I'm not dead. I was never dead.

Chinese Elvis Right. Great. You look well.

Louise I just left, you see. I'd had enough. But my mother told everyone I was dead.

Chinese Elvis Oh . . . What did you die of?

Louise That's a good question, Elvis. I don't know. I'll have to ask her . . . I've been away for ten years. You'd think they'd be pleased to see me.

Chinese Elvis It must be a shock.

Louise Suppose. Anyway, why don't you sing something?

Chinese Elvis What?

Louise I don't want to be blamed for wrecking the party. 'Suspicious Minds'. Sing that one.

Chinese Elvis I don't know it all.

Louise I'll help you out.

Chinese Elvis (*looking at his tape recorder*) I'm not sure.

Louise Oh come on. We'll tempt them all back in here. Work your magic, Elvis. Besides I feel like a dance.

Louise helps herself to a drink.

Chinese Elvis (*tentatively*)
    We're caught in a trap
    I can't walk out –

Louise That's it, Elvis.

Chinese Elvis
    Because I love you too much, baby –

Louise Give it some welly, Elvis. Come on.

Chinese Elvis
    Why can't you see
    What you're doing to me
    When you don't believe a word I'm saying.

Josie watches through the patio doors. Louise sings backing vocals.

Chinese Elvis
    We can't go on together with suspicious minds

Louise
    Suspicious minds

Chinese Elvis
    And we can't build our dreams
    On suspicious minds

Louise (*prompts Chinese Elvis*)
So if an old friend I know –

Chinese Elvis
– I know
Stops by to say hello
Would I still see suspicion in your eye

Chinese Elvis
Here we go again
Asking where I've been,

Louise
Ahh. Ahh. Ahh.
You can't see –

Chinese Elvis
The tears
I feel I'm crying

Louise
Yes I'm crying –

Chinese Elvis/Louise
We can't go on together
With suspicious minds
Suspicious minds
And we can't build our dreams
On suspicious minds –

Josie enters. They don't notice her at first.

Louise (*prompts Chinese Elvis again*)
Oh let our love survive-
Oh dry the tears from your eyes
Don't let a good thing die
'Cos you know honey I would never lie to you

Chinese Elvis
Ooh, Ooh, yeah, yeah
We're caught in a trap –

Louise Oh. Here she is, Elvis. Look, we can ask her now. How did I die, Mother? Elvis and me really want to know.

Josie Don't do this, Shelly-Louise.

Louise No, no, come on, Mother. I don't mind. Was it in a car crash? Or did I have cancer? Oh no, did I lose all my hair? Did I throw myself off the Town Hall? Did I drown in the bath?

Josie I haven't got the strength for this.

Louise Did I drink weed killer? Was it very sudden? Did I drown on a school trip? Or was it a freak electrocution? Come on, Mother, spill the beans, what did you tell everyone? How did I die?

Chinese Elvis (*switching off his music*) I think that's enough of that one.

Josie You choked on your own vomit.

Louise (*taken aback*) What?

Josie You heard me.

Chinese Elvis I think I left something in the bathroom.

Louise (*trying to hide her hurt*) You shock me, Mother. That's a terrible way to go, don't you think Elvis?

Chinese Elvis Yeah, yeah. I don't know.

Josie She said I made her sick, sick to her stomach, Elvis.

Chinese Elvis Right.

Louise Did I get a funeral? Surely I did. Never one to miss an occasion to dress up, were you, Mother?

Josie It was the Monday. The Monday after I said you'd died. Four months after you'd gone. I got up and I went to Blackpool for the day.

Chinese Elvis I love Blackpool.

Josie I think Blackpool's one of the most depressing places on this earth.

Louise Did you wear black?

Josie I wore navy. Black wouldn't have been quite right.

Louise And you cried for your poor dead Shelly-Louise?

Josie Something like that.

Louise What about Brenda-Marie? Didn't she want to go to my funeral?

Josie I told her your body had gone for medical research.

Louise Poor kid.

Josie We had a ceremony in the garden.

Louise Like when Hammy the Hamster died.

Josie We said some prayers and then we erected a tent. She wanted a place of her own where she could always go off and think about her sister.

Louise So I had a good send-off.

Josie I didn't send you off. You left of your own accord. It was so hot that summer. I couldn't get any relief.

Chinese Elvis I'll pop back in a bit, shall I? See if you're ready for another song.

Louise You look old, Mother. She looks old, doesn't she, Elvis?

Chinese Elvis Well, no, no, I wouldn't say old.

Josie It's all right, Elvis, I am old.

Louise I can't believe you said I'd died. Can you believe that, Elvis?

Chinese Elvis Well, I –

Josie Brenda-Marie was on at me every day, 'Where's she gone, where's our Shelly-Louise?'. I didn't know what to say to her, Elvis.

Chinese Elvis No.

Louise She could have said she didn't know where I was, couldn't she?

Chinese Elvis Yeah.

Josie You said you'd never come back. You said that I was no longer your Mother, that you didn't care what happened to me and Brenda-Marie. Terrible things. You said you'd never ever come back. I didn't want her to live in hope. We had to mourn you like you were dead. It was easier that way.

Louise It was easier without me.

Josie I didn't say that.

Louise But it was.

Chinese Elvis If you'll just excuse me a minute.

Josie I saw this documentary on the tele, Elvis. It was about an earthquake in Mexico. Terrible it was. The city was flattened. Thousands of people died. And they were talking to this man – he was a rescue worker and he said they heard this crying under the rubble. And they dug down and found this child – still alive – crying. And the child was in his Mother's arms. Still wrapped up in her arms. But the thing was the Mother was dead, so they tried to lift the boy out of her arms but they couldn't do it, she was gripping him so tight. So do you know what they did? They sawed her arms off. They had to cut the Mother's arms off to get at the crying boy.

Chinese Elvis That's bad.

Louise Why are you saying this, Mother?

Josie They had to cut my arms off too, Elvis, when my daughter left.

Chinese Elvis Really?

Louise Metaphorically speaking.

Josie What?

Louise Well, they clearly didn't cut your arms off. Although it might have gone down a storm at work, mightn't it, Mother? Torture courtesy of glamorous Bolton amputee. What do you think, Elvis? Some of the kinky ones would love that, wouldn't they?

Chinese Elvis Yeah. I dunno.

Josie How did you get to be so hard?

Louise My Mother's a prostitute. I learned it from her.

Chinese Elvis Right. I think I'll find Lionel.

Josie No, you're all right, Elvis. I haven't got the strength for this, Shelly-Louise. I'm sorry but I haven't.

She gets up to go.

Louise Where are you going?

Josie You're right, I'm too old. And I've had enough. We can't go through all this again. I don't understand why you went and I don't understand why you've come back.

Louise Afraid to face it, Mother?

Josie You left us in the lurch, Shelly-Louise. Not a word for ten years. And just because you've decided it's time to come back, doesn't mean we can all dance to your tune. I'm sorry. (*She exits.*)

Chinese Elvis I think I'll just go and try another costume. I don't think this one is working out.

Louise I'm sorry Elvis. This is nothing to do with you.

Chinese Elvis No.

Louise It never comes out right.

Chinese Elvis What?

Louise The things you mean to say.

SCENE TWO

Someone knocks on the door five times.

Louise Come in. Come in. Come in. For Christ's sake.

She goes and opens the door. Martha is poised for more knocking.

Martha I've been saying the rosary for you and your Mother.

Louise I think we'll need more than that. You can come in. We've finished.

Martha Hello Elvis.

Chinese Elvis I'm just going.

Martha Oh no. You can't go. I'm sure if I was having a crisis I'd want Elvis close at hand.

Chinese Elvis Yeah. Well I'm going to try the fat years. See if I have any more luck with them.

They look at him. He exits.

Louise Well.

Martha You have a lot to be grateful for.

Louise Do you think so?

Martha You're not dead for a start.

Louise No. I ought to thank my lucky stars.

Martha And your Mother. You ought to thank your Mother.

Louise Mmm. Do you have children?

Martha I haven't been blessed with children myself. But I was a member of the Catholic Mothers' Union.

Louise How did you manange that?

Martha I got in on a technicality. A loophole in canon law. Besides they needed someone who was good at sewing.

Louise Oh.

Martha Gowns for stillborn babies.

Louise What?

Martha We each had a duty. Mine was making gowns for stillborn babies.

Louise How sad.

Martha Yes, but it was a gift too. I made them beautiful, intricate, full of detail. I didn't want to make them any less so, just because the child was – I liked doing it. It helped the parents I think.

Louise But you don't do it any more?

Martha I got thrown out.

Louise Why?

Martha I had a set-to with a lay member of the Knights of Columbia. Because I wouldn't give up counting for Lent.

Louise You're a funny lot, aren't you?

Martha What?

Louise It must be difficult to be a practising Catholic and still be on the game.

Martha I beg your pardon?

Louise Is Lionel one of yours or one of hers?

Martha One, two, three, four, five. I really don't –

Louise What's your speciality? Do you whip them with your hair?

Martha One, two, three, I clean, four, five – I clean –

Louise The saucy maid thing. No offence but isn't that a bit seventies?

Martha Five, ten, fifteen, twenty, twenty-five –

Louise Apparently my Mother wows them with her honey tongue. Gets them going with her vocabulary. I mean I've got to hand it to her for keeping it up for so long. She can't look good in the bondage gear anymore.

Martha Thirty, thirty-five, forty –

> *Lionel enters. During the next, Martha continues to count under her breath and develops an alarming array of nervous tics.*

Lionel I think Elvis may have done a bunk. This is probably a bit of a pressure gig for him. Is everything all right?

Louise We were just discussing the tricks of the trade. What's your thing, Lionel? Lots of rubber? No I'd have you down as more of a nappy man.

Martha (*with difficulty*) Mr Trills is a dry cleaner.

Louise Oh I bet my Mother gives you gold service. A nice hand finish.

Martha He cleans and I clean. We both clean.

Louise Mmm. Yes. A very nice line in French polishing.

Martha Mrs Botting is a counsellor.

Louise That's one word for it. Anyway if you'll excuse me, there's something I need to do. Have fun. (*to Lionel*) Good luck, Lionel. I bet she goes like the clappers.

She exits.

SCENE THREE

Lionel Miss Clear, I –

Martha Five, ten, fifteen, twenty, twenty-five, thirty – This is very bad. When I start doing my five times table, this is a sign that things have got very bad.

Lionel Josie's a good woman. She just felt it was easier not to tell you.

Martha She's a jezebel?

Lionel She's a dominatrix. A Madam, yes.

Martha I'm here under false pretences.

Lionel Please don't go, Miss Clear.

Martha Answer me one thing. Are you one of her –

Lionel Yes, yes I am. But she's a friend too. I don't do it that often and when I do, it's more the dressing up –

Martha I knew there was something funny about you.

Lionel Let me explain. Miss Clear –

Martha You're a pervert!

Lionel And you're an obsessive-compulsive.

Martha Two wrongs don't make a right, Mr Trills. Excuse me –

Lionel We have to see this through.

Martha See what through?

Lionel There's a rapport between us. Admit it. You feel it too.

Martha I don't like you.

Lionel Why not?

Martha I don't like the cut of your gib, Mister.

Lionel Let's just talk about this.

Martha I can't stay in this whorehouse a minute longer.

Lionel Where are you going? Martha?

Martha I'm handing my notice in. I will no longer clean a den of sin and iniquity. I'm going home.

Lionel But why? What are you going back to?

Martha The straight and narrow. That's what I'm going back to.

Lionel You're lonely. And I'm lonely.

Martha Now that's where you're wrong. I relish my own company. I'm the best company I know. Excuse me.

Lionel I want to confess to you, Martha.

Martha I suggest you don't. The urge to confess in this day and age is far too strong.

Lionel I'm sad and I'm lonely and I visit a Madam because I like to dress up in women's clothing.

Martha You what?

Lionel Have done since I was a boy. I just like the feel of a skirt. The swish. The air between my legs.

Martha Hold it right there, Mr Trills. You really aren't doing yourself any favours.

Lionel I don't think it's evil, Martha. I wish I had a wife. I wish I had kids. But I don't and going to Josie is the best company I get.

Martha I bet it is.

Lionel I'm not talking about the sex. I'm sorry, I know how this all sounds. I want to be frank with you.

Martha I don't need to hear any more, Mr Trills.

Lionel Lionel. Please call me Lionel.

Martha Why should I?

Lionel It's my name.

Martha What sort of name is Lionel?

Lionel Jewish. It's a Jewish name.

Martha Holy Mary Mother of God. I'm stuck in a whorehouse with a Jew who likes to wear women's clothing. What have I done to deserve this? I know your sort, Lionel. You'll be trying to shave off my hair and make me wear one of those wig things.

Lionel Sheitels.

Martha I don't want to hear your filth.

Lionel I was brought up Jewish but I don't practise anymore.

Martha Oh my God! A lapsed Jew. We're really running the gamut this evening.

Lionel Catholics don't have the monopoly over lapsing, you know. Besides Jesus was a Jew.

Martha I really don't have the time for a theological debate, now if you'll excuse me –

Lionel No I won't.

Martha I beg your pardon.

Lionel I'm not letting you go.

Martha Why not?

Lionel I'll stop you counting. I'll fill your life so full you won't have time to count.

Martha Please don't go all gung-ho on me, Mr Trills.

Lionel I want to dance with you, Martha. I bet you're a smashing dancer. I want to bring you forward to glorious technicolour.

Martha You really fancy your chances don't you?

Lionel I want you to fling your shoulders back. I want to dance the tango with you.

Martha And will you be wearing a dress?

Lionel I want you to walk barefoot in the snow. I want to hear you laugh in eight different languages.

Martha I'm very sorry, Mr Trills but I have no intention of venturing out into the snow without the benefit of shoes and I'm not multilingual and anyway I'm leaving. Be so good as to tell Mrs Botting that I am never going to darken her door again. Good night.

Martha exits. At the same time the Chinese Elvis enters from another door. He is wearing an Elvis costume from Elvis' last years, with padding.

Lionel Martha! Wait! It's freezing out there. You'll catch your death. (*He looks for Martha's coat.*)

Chinese Elvis I've been looking for you, Lionel.

Lionel Yeah. Not right now, lad.

Chinese Elvis I'm not having a very good time.

Lionel No, you're not the only one.

Chinese Elvis Nobody's interested in hearing me sing.

Lionel Well, that's showbiz. Do you know what Martha's coat looks like?

Chinese Elvis There's weird shit going on in this house. I think I might call it a night.

Lionel No, I'm going to need you later on. That's a good costume.

Chinese Elvis I'm representing the late years.

Lionel Are you wearing padding?

Chinese Elvis A bit.

Lionel Nice touch. Now, Tim, I'm on a bit of a mission. I've got to deliver a coat to a damsel in distress. You just sit tight and I won't be long.

Chinese Elvis Yeah but –

Lionel I'll make it worth your while. Help yourself to a catastrophe.

Lionel rushes out the front door after Martha. The Chinese Elvis goes over to the mirror. He starts to sing to himself.

Chinese Elvis
  Love letters straight from your heart
  Keep us so near while apart
  I'm not alone in the night
  When I can have all the love you write –

  Brenda-Marie appears from outside and watches him.
  He doesn't see her until right at the end.

Brenda-Marie You're sad, Chinese Elvis.

Chinese Elvis Yeah. Thanks.

  Brenda-Marie enters.

Brenda-Marie Nobody's come to find me. To see if I'm all right. I've been in my tent for about three hours.

Chinese Elvis Your Mum and your sister are upstairs I think.

Brenda-Marie I'm not going to them.

Chinese Elvis Right.

Brenda-Marie The way I see it, Chinese Elvis, my sister died and my Mam told me she was dead and I cried enough tears to fill a thousand ice trays and now she comes back so she either didn't die or she did die and this girl's just a Shelly-Louise impersonator and anyway my Mam told me a big bad fib so I'm not going running to them.

Chinese Elvis No.

Brenda-Marie It's definitely going to snow out there.

Chinese Elvis How do you know?

Brenda-Marie I can feel it in my bones.

Chinese Elvis You must have an old soul.

Brenda-Marie You what?

Chinese Elvis Some people are just born full of ancient wisdom. You must be one of them.

Brenda-Marie Do you think so?

Chinese Elvis Yeah.

Brenda-Marie Holy Jo says it's too cold to snow. That's mad, isn't it? I mean what does that mean? How can it be too cold to snow?

Chinese Elvis Perhaps it's like when people say they're too tired to sleep.

Brenda-Marie I'm never too tired to sleep.

Chinese Elvis Or like when people are really really upset but they can't cry. They'd like to cry but they can't. They're beyond tears. Maybe it's like that. The sky is just beyond snow.

Brenda-Marie Yes. I suppose so. Do you know, if my Mam and my sister come down now and I don't feel like talking to them, I'm going to say I'm very sorry but I'm too cold to snow right now. I'm beyond snow.

Chinese Elvis And if they ask me to sing I'm going to tell them, I'm sorry I'm too cold to snow as well.

Brenda-Marie Good.

Chinese Elvis That's settled then.

Brenda-Marie Is it cold where you come from, Chinese Elvis?

Chinese Elvis I come from Whalley Range.

Brenda-Marie No your China home.

Chinese Elvis Vietnam. I was born in Vietnam.

Brenda-Marie Was it cold?

Chinese Elvis I come from the North. It can be very cold and it can be very hot. But I don't remember it.

Brenda-Marie Why did you leave?

Chinese Elvis I don't know – I was a little boy. I came with my parents on a boat. We were boat people.

Brenda-Marie You were a boat boy. A Vietnamese boat boy.

Chinese Elvis Yes, I was.

Brenda-Marie But did you always want to be an Elvis when you grew up?

Chinese Elvis No. But I've always liked the way he sang.

Brenda-Marie Do you like being an Elvis?

Chinese Elvis I don't really know yet. When I'm the Chinese Elvis I would say on the whole that people much prefer me to when I'm Timothy Wong.

Brenda-Marie Why?

Chinese Elvis I suppose that's because to them I'm an icon of the twentieth century instead of some skinny chinky. Last week I had to do this hen party. And all these women went wild. They threw their knickers at me. I think they were having a laugh. But I mean they wouldn't have thrown their knickers if I was just Timothy Wong, would they?

Brenda-Marie Did you like it when they threw their pants?

Chinese Elvis Not particularly. They weren't nice – Marks and Spencer pants that had gone grey in the wash. I think if I'd been the real Elvis, I'd have been a bit insulted. Then I thought it was sad, the way they all came up afterwards and scrabbled around on the floor for them.

Brenda-Marie I would never be a pant-thrower.

Chinese Elvis No, I didn't think you would.

Brenda-Marie Will you be my boyfriend?

Chinese Elvis No.

Brenda-Marie Oh, okay.

Chinese Elvis I'm sorry.

Brenda-Marie No, I'm not that bothered. Sometimes I think it would be nice to have a boyfriend because most people do. But most of the time I think I'd rather have Sky Television.

Chinese Elvis The thing is, Brenda-Marie, if I was going to have a girlfriend I would almost certainly choose someone like you.

Brenda-Marie That's good to know, Chinese Elvis.

Chinese Elvis But, well, I'm not that fussed about girls.

Brenda-Marie Oh.

Chinese Elvis It gets a bit tricky especially when I'm the Chinese Elvis because I'm supposed to be like this sex symbol to all these women.

Brenda-Marie But what you really want is an Elvis to call your own.

Chinese Elvis I think I'd rather have a John Lennon. He's more my type.

Brenda-Marie If Elvis walked in right now, how would you feel?

Chinese Elvis I don't know. I'd probably feel a bit over-dressed.

Brenda-Marie I'd be cross. You can't just go off and pretend to be dead. It's not fair on the rest of us.

Chinese Elvis Why not?

Brenda-Marie Because when you think that someone is dead, you think about them every day. It's like they're more alive to you because you can't stop thinking about them. You can't just send them down the shops for ten minutes. You can't go on holiday to have a break from them. You have to think about them. And your Mam thinks about them and when she looks at you she's thinking about the dead one. And then you find out they're not dead and you think what a waste of time. I could have been thinking about something nice for ten years and going on holiday and eating ice-cream instead of feeling sad sad sad for an alive dead person.

Chinese Elvis But maybe your sister had her reasons.

Pause.

Brenda-Marie Why, do you think she couldn't live with me?

Chinese Elvis I don't know. Maybe she had to get away for a bit. To find herself.

Brenda-Marie Why couldn't she find herself in Bolton?

Chinese Elvis I don't know. People have to go on long journeys sometimes. I had to come from Vietnam to Whalley Range to find myself as Timothy Wong. Then in a way I had to go to Las Vegas to find myself as the Chinese Elvis.

Brenda-Marie The furthest I've gone is to my tent.

Chinese Elvis Well, you're full of ancient wisdom, you see. You don't have far to travel in this life, because you already know who you are. But none of it matters. The main thing is she's come back to you. That's a pretty brave thing for her to do.

Brenda-Marie Yes I suppose so. It's nice talking to you, Timothy Wong.

Chinese Elvis You're the only one that thinks so this evening.

Brenda-Marie I prefer you to Elvis. You should be a Timothy Wong impersonator.

Chinese Elvis No I don't think so.

Louise enters in domination gear, with cuffs etc hanging from her belt. She carries a whip.

Louise Brenda-Marie!

Brenda-Marie stares at her sister.

Brenda-Marie No! I'm too cold to snow. (*She runs out.*)

SCENE FIVE

Louise I'm Mrs Popular tonight. Hello again Elvis.

Chinese Elvis (*uncomfortable*) Oh hello. All right?

Louise Still trying to find someone to sing to?

Chinese Elvis Nobody seems very interested in hearing me sing.

Louise Elvis has had his day, hasn't he?

Chinese Elvis Yeah. Well. I'll just go and see if she's all right.

Louise Sing to me.

Chinese Elvis What?

Louise You heard me.

Chinese Elvis I already did.

Louise It's not a request. It's an order.

Chinese Elvis I don't really feel up to it.

Louise Get down on your knees.

Chinese Elvis What?

Louise Adopt slave position. Do it now.

Chinese Elvis Is this a joke?

She cracks the whip

Louise Of course it's not. I'm telling you to impersonate Elvis.

Chinese Elvis I can't do it if I'm forced.

Louise Of course you can. Get down on all fours.

She pushes him down. She puts her foot on his back. She forces his head back.

Sing, Elvis. I'm ordering you to sing.

Chinese Elvis I can't. You're restricting my vocal chords.

Louise Come on. And it better be just like Elvis. Or there will be hell to pay.

Chinese Elvis It's very difficult when you can't do the movements as well. I don't think Elvis sang from this position as a rule.

Louise Less of the lip from you Elvis. I am your Madam and I've given you a command. Be Elvis for me now.

Chinese Elvis Anything in particular?

Louise You're so insolent. I think this calls for a swift course of treatment.

She grabs his hair.

Chinese Elvis Oy. That hurts.

Louise You have to choose. You're lucky your Madam is giving you freedom of choice.

Chinese Elvis How about 'She's the Devil in Disguise'?

Louise Don't be cocky. It doesn't suit you. (*She digs her stiletto into his back.*)

Chinese Elvis Ow. Ow. Please. This is not my idea of fun.

Louise Sing something flattering. Pay homage to your Madam. (*She starts grinding her foot.*)

Chinese Elvis Okay. Okay.
    When no-one else can understand me –

Louise You don't sound like him. You're not a bit like Elvis. Do you know that? You've got no future. Start again. Come on, make me think you're Elvis, China boy.

Chinese Elvis
    When no-one else can understand me –

Louise No-one understands you, Elvis? Poor Elvis. It's okay. I'm here. I'm very understanding. (*She turns him over and sits on him.*)

Chinese Elvis
    When everything I do is wrong –

Louise Naughty, naughty, Elvis. Always getting things wrong. We'll have to punish you.

Chinese Elvis
    You give me hope and consolation
    You give me strength to carry on

The thing is –

Louise You want me. But you can't have me, Elvis.

Chinese Elvis No. That's fine. I think you're very nice and everything.

She pulls his hair.

Louise You have to sing for your supper here, Elvis.

Chinese Elvis
And you're always there to lend a hand –

Louise Yes I am.

Chinese Elvis
In everything I do –

Louise I'm always ready with a helping hand, Elvis. (*She touches him suggestively.*)

Chinese Elvis No please. In any other circumstance, believe me –

Louise Don't stop singing. Convince me you're Elvis.

Chinese Elvis
That's the wonder, the wonder of you –

Josie enters during the last.

Josie What the – ? Elvis, are you all right there, lad?

Chinese Elvis I'm not sure.

Louise What do you think, Mam? Am I a chip off the old block?

Josie Where did you get those clothes?

Chinese Elvis Can I get up please? You're squashing me.

Louise They're yours. From years ago. Don't you recognise them? They fit me perfectly.

Chinese Elvis I've got to get changed.

Louise I wanted to know what it feels like. I thought I was rather good. What did you think, Elvis?

Chinese Elvis What?

Louise Was I good?

Chinese Elvis In what sense?

Louise Did you feel – dominated?

Chinese Elvis Oh yes, definitely.

Louise Did I turn you on?

Chinese Elvis In what way?

Louise What do you mean, in what way? There's only one way, isn't there?

Chinese Elvis Oh. Well. I'm a bit restricted in this costume. You were very good though.

Louise You're a hard act to follow but I always knew I had it in me, Mam.

Chinese Elvis To tell you the truth, this isn't really my scene. A couple of my friends would be really into it. I could give you their numbers.

Louise It's funny. I would never dream of doing this, Mother. At home. It makes me feel a bit sick to tell the truth. I'm really very conservative. Lights off and everything. But it's weird, isn't it? I can see how you might get to enjoy it.

Josie You look –

Louise I look like you used to.

Josie No you don't.

Louise Yes I do. This is what you looked like, Mam. When we were little.

Josie Take it off. Right now.

Louise Why, don't you like it?

Josie I should have thrown all that old stuff out.

Louise Doesn't it suit me? What do you think, Elvis? Does it suit me?

Josie Let him go, Louise. He's not enjoying it.

Chinese Elvis Yeah. It really suits you.

Josie It's not right. If they don't enjoy it, it's cruel.

Chinese Elvis But I'm not into girls *per se*.

Louise Don't you dare speak unless spoken too. (*She cracks the whip. Pause.*)

Josie Give me the whip, Shelly-Louise.

Louise What? No.

Josie If you're going to do it, do it right, Shelly-Louise. You must wield the whip with conviction. You've got to be cruel but with the hint of a kink, you've got to be subtle, you've got to be devastating. You're apologising for it. They smell weakness. The dominatrix must be brisk and masterful. You can't just do it willy-nilly. Tell him what you're going to do. Tell him why he must be punished. Right then. Call yourself Elvis do you?

Chinese Elvis What?

Josie cracks the whip.

Josie Speak up, Elvis. You're stimulating my wrath.

Chinese Elvis Sorry, Josie?

Josie MADAM Josie.

Chinese Elvis What?

Josie I find your demeanour woefully inadequate, Elvis.

Chinese Elvis What are you doing?

She ties him to a chair.

Josie Give me the manacles, Shelly-Louise. You have to be swift with them. Take them by surprise with your artefacts.

Chinese Elvis What? Please don't do this. Mind my costume. You'll fray the cuffs.

Josie Hush up, you big girl's blouse. We've got plenty of costumes here. Transformation is a specialty. Right. Why haven't you learned all the songs?

Chinese Elvis I know quite a few.

Josie Do you now? We'll see about that. Stuck on you.

Chinese Elvis What?

Josie Sing it.

Chinese Elvis Um –

Josie Wooden heart. Come on. Everyone knows that one.

Chinese Elvis You're putting me under pressure here.

Josie Teddy bear. Put a chain around his neck and lead him anywhere.

Chinese Elvis Please, Josie. Madam Josie. I do know the songs, really, I –

Josie Enough of this persiflage, Elvis. Do you know something, Elvis? You're nothing but a hound dog. I bet you've never caught a rabbit. You're no friend of mine.

Chinese Elvis No, please. Don't be cruel.

Josie Don't be cruel, my favourite. Sing it then.

Louise All right, Josie. You've made your point.

Josie Why are you wearing padding, Elvis? Trying to escape your punishment?

Chinese Elvis No, I –

Josie This calls for drastic measures, Elvis. Men are simple creatures you see, Shelly-Louise. I'm going to wreak havoc on you, Elvis. I'm going to give you the works. I know you hanker, Elvis. But I shall satisfy your hankering. I shall set about you with vigour. What do you say to a good old-fashioned drubbing? Yes. I'm going to put you on the hot seat, smack you till you smart. I'm going to feather you, leather you, smother you in fondant. I'm going to ride you pillion, kindle your winkle, rump you till you sizzle, stir you to jelly, custard you to cream. You see, Shelly-Louise, all you really need in this business is a dictionary and a packet of Kleenex. Is that what you want, Elvis?

Chinese Elvis I'm not sure.

Louise I never want to be like you, Mother.

Chinese Elvis Can I go now please?

Louise Never ever.

Josie I did it all for you and Brenda-Marie. So's you'd have the best.

Chinese Elvis I'm gonna have to ask for time and a half for this you know.

Josie I had to bring them up on my own, Elvis. Their father wouldn't have anything to do with them. A drunken old sod. Shirked his responsibilities. The original bloody Bolton wanderer. Do you know the closest I ever got to love, Elvis? In the back of a Ford Capri in Oldham. But I'm not complaining. Some people get all the love. They get the Trevi Fountain and the Bridge of Sighs and some people get a Ford Capri in the home of the Tubular Bandage.

Chinese Elvis Do you mind undoing these cuffs?

Josie I did it from home, Elvis. I didn't stand on street corners.

Chinese Elvis They're digging into me.

Louise She makes it sound like a lovely little cottage industry, doesn't she?

Chinese Elvis And I need a wee.

Louise She never faces up to things, Elvis. For a hooker she really lives in Cloud-Cuckoo Land.

Josie Where does she expect me to live, Elvis? This is how I've survived. I'm sixty today. I'm riddled with arthritis and I'm on the list for a hip and I haven't slept right in ten years. I'm amazed I'm as intact as I am.

Louise And I'm thirty, Elvis. And I don't know who I am. I've had to change my name. I've had to re-invent myself.

Josie Well you've done a good job. I don't recognise you at all.

Louise I'm very good at transformations. It's my Mother's line of business.

Josie So why come back Shelly-Louise? If you hate everything I stand for.

Louise I don't know. It was a mistake.

Chinese Elvis (*changing tack*) No it wasn't.

Louise What?

Chinese Elvis You must have a very good reason. To come back now.

Josie Who asked you?

Chinese Elvis The pair of you have been miserable for ten years and now you're just going to balls it up again.

Josie You stay out of this Elvis.

Chinese Elvis I thought women were supposed to be good at communicating.

Josie I'm warning you.

Chinese Elvis The only person with any sense in this family is Brenda-Marie.

Louise I want to get married.

Chinese Elvis There we go then. It's out at last.

Josie What?

Louise Somebody's asked me. A good man. He's looking to give me the Trevi Fountain and the Bridge of Sighs –

Josie Shelly-Louise –

Louise But there's something stopping me. This place. You.

Chinese Elvis But you came back to sort it out.

Louise I had this – dream – that maybe I could get married, that maybe none of this mattered, who I was and where I came from and that maybe even my Mother would want to give me away. And Brenda-Marie could be my bridesmaid. But my Mother told everyone I was dead. She just dispensed with me –

Josie That's not true, Shelly-Louise.

Louise Louise. My name is Louise now.

Josie Louise, I –

Louise You can't even be happy for me, can you, Mother? Because you never had it, I'm not allowed to have it either. I'd better go.

She exits.

Chinese Elvis Can you untie me now?

Josie Yes, sorry lad.

Chinese Elvis Call yourself a dominatrix?

Josie I've lost the will, Elvis. Here, I'll get you some Fuller's Earth.

Chinese Elvis It's okay.

Josie It's good for chafing.

Chinese Elvis Go after her.

Josie She doesn't want me to.

Chinese Elvis Yes she does.

Josie I don't know what to say to her. I haven't got the words.

Chinese Elvis Yes you have. Tell her why you want her back.

Josie I can't.

Chinese Elvis That's not a request. That's an order, Madam Josie.

Josie If I lost her again, I couldn't bear it.

Chinese Elvis I know a song about that. I could do it for you.

Josie No, no, Elvis you're right, I'd better get my skates on.

Chinese Elvis Yeah.

She exits. Chinese Elvis sighs, pours himself a soft drink. Martha enters.

SCENE SIX

Martha Oh Elvis. Have you seen my coat?

Chinese Elvis I'm not singing for anybody else.

Martha I'm sure that's a blessed relief to all concerned. Now have you seen my coat? It's freezing out there.

Chinese Elvis No.

Martha Now where is it? One, two, three, four, five. One, two, three, four, five. One, two, three, four, five.

Lionel enters. Martha doesn't notice him at first.

Chinese Elvis Why do you count?

Martha Oh Lord, not another one. What is this sudden obsession with my counting?

Lionel We want to know, Martha. Why do you?

Martha (*she jumps*) Oh God. Where did you come from?

Lionel I've been following you. Here's your coat.

Martha Elvis. Ring the police. I knew he was a stalker. What are you waiting for? He's probably about to expose himself to me.

Chinese Elvis Probably. Nothing would surprise me any more. Now I'm just going to say goodbye to Brenda-Marie and then I'm off.

Lionel Oh no you're not. I've paid you till midnight. Besides Martha and I are going to need you.

Martha What?

Lionel Martha here has promised me a dance so we're going to need musical accompaniment.

Martha I have done nothing of the sort. Ring the police, Elvis.

Lionel Yes go on, Elvis. Ring the police. That's 999. Three numbers which if you invert them become 666.

Martha (*puts her hands over her ears*) No, no, you evil little man.

Lionel Tell them they've got to come to Bolton. Tell them they'll find Bolton at the end of the A666. Also known as the Devil's Highway.

Martha One, two, three, four, five. One, two, three, four, five.

Lionel There's no point putting your hands over your ears, Martha. Me and Elvis are going to sort you out. Tonight is kill or cure night.

Chinese Elvis You can count me out. I'm not singing any more.

Lionel I'm sure Martha here would be very happy to count you out. I on the other hand may need your assistance. Now Martha, answer Elvis' question. Why do you count?

Martha Because I have to.

Lionel Not good enough.

Martha Why do you dress in women's clothing?

Chinese Elvis What?

Martha Oh Elvis, did he forget to mention to you that he's a cross-dressing pervert?

Lionel It must have slipped my mind, Elvis. Forgive me.

Chinese Elvis That's okay.

Lionel I dress in women's clothing because I enjoy it. You should try it, Elvis.

Chinese Elvis I might. I know I'm getting sick to the back teeth of Elvis. I might try my hand at Shirley Bassey.

Martha I count because I enjoy it.

Lionel No you don't.

Martha I've done this ever since I can remember.

Lionel So?

Martha Counting reminds me that I'm alive. Count to ten, my Mother used to say. When they hit you and knock you down. When they provoke you. Count to ten. Every time someone ignores me or is rude to me or jostles me in the street. I am so constantly provoked I haven't got time for ten, so I count to five and I know I'm real, I'm still here. Numbers take away the pain.

Lionel Like the number six.

Martha Don't – Some numbers are inherently evil. Don't ask me why, they just are. You don't need to worry about me. I used to be much worse than I am. I used to have to convert everything into Roman numerals.

Chinese Elvis That must have taken a long time.

Martha It did, Elvis.

Lionel But what if you didn't count, what would happen?

Martha Something bad. Something bad would happen.

Brenda-Marie enters in a flurry from outside.

Brenda-Marie Chinese Elvis, I require your urgent assistance outside.

Martha You see! What is it, Brenda-Marie? What's happened?

Brenda-Marie It's nothing to do with you, Holy Jo.

Chinese Elvis I'm right behind you.

Lionel But I'm going to need you.

Martha You're in great demand, Elvis.

Brenda-Marie I need him most. Come on Timothy Wong.

Brenda-Marie and the Chinese Elvis exit. Martha goes to follow them.

Lionel No you don't.

Martha Mr Trills. Brenda-Marie is obviously on the verge of a crisis. I need to help her.

Lionel She'll be all right. She's got Elvis with her.

Martha You don't understand, do you? We could all be inches away from disaster. Have you read the obituaries lately?

Lionel You should be glad, thankful to be alive.

Martha I am. I count my blessings. I count them very carefully every night.

Lionel It's no way to live, Martha.

Martha I don't think someone who gets pleasure out of wearing women's panty-girdles is in a position to judge.

Lionel You're always peering off cliffs instead of looking up and exalting.

Martha I exalt all the time but you just have to be careful.

Lionel You're living your life all hunched up.

Martha At least I don't visit a Madam to get my kicks.

Lionel You're living your life in fear.

Martha No, I'm living my life in suspicion. It's very different.

Lionel You should throw open your chest, throw wide your arms –

Martha Are you a lesbian?

Lionel (*suddenly weary*) No Martha. I'm not. (*Pause.*) Do you want a drink? I need a catastrophe.

Martha It's all a catastrophe. Everything is a catastrophe.

Pause.

Lionel (*he hands her a glass*) Here. It's hard when you go on and on and nobody notices your potential.

Martha Speak for yourself.

Lionel I am, Martha. People don't take a blind bit of notice of you when you're a dry cleaner. On the whole people have never taken any notice of me. I'm short and I'm bald and I hand them a ticket for clean clothes next Thursday. That's how much I figure. I'm very easy to overlook. But the clothes speak to me. The dirty clothes full of stains. People have no idea what they're giving away when they hand me their duvets to clean, intimate details of their lives, dirt they want erased. But do you know what? I love the mess because it means people are living their lives. I hate it when you go into a house and you feel like you can't sit on the seats, you can't walk on the carpet, you can't piss in the toilet. I want to see a house that's lived in, a coat that's worn, a church that's prayed in, all of us have got a use, Martha, all of us.

Pause. She sits.

Martha I don't want to be like this any more.

Lionel I know you don't.

Martha I wanted to be a nurse. I wanted to have a child. I wanted to go to Graceland. And it's all passed me by.

Lionel No it hasn't. It needn't.

Martha People look at me like I'm a loonie. I am a loonie.

Lionel Look at this glass, Martha. My Mother used to love crystal. She said it made the drink taste better. But what is it really? A piece of glass that has been cut many times. A glass that's made up of flaws.

Martha What?

Lionel I know you feel scarred because I feel scarred too. But I look at you and I see – top quality crystal. I'd rather drink from you than a plastic beaker any day.

Martha Please don't –

Lionel Do you know something, Martha? You haven't counted hardly at all this evening.

Martha I must have done.

Lionel Or washed your hands.

Martha No?

Lionel You've been too busy living.

Martha Why are you bothering with me, Lionel?

Lionel Because you've got a lot to offer.

Martha Really I haven't. I'm a deeply unfortunate woman.

Lionel I've got an urge to reclaim unfortunate women.

Martha I'm sorry, Lionel. I just can't.

Lionel Can't what?

Martha This. That. The other. Here. Now. Ever. With you. Sorry.

Lionel You don't find me attractive enough.

Martha It's not that.

Lionel Then what?

Pause. Martha counts softly to herself. She cries silently.

Lionel I'd better go.

Pause. He goes to exit.

Martha No. Please. Lionel. (*quietly*) Have you seen those girls? The girls in town on a Friday night. No more than sixteen some of them. In their best bib and tucker. Well actually, it's hardly that is it? Wouldn't cover a flea. Half a bib and no tucker to speak of. In their big bovver boots and the sparkle round their eyes. And some of them are in army gear, with their bosoms hanging out and they look at you like they're about to karate chop the living daylights out of you. And I think, they'll catch their death – I would – but they don't. They've got thermostats in their boots. And I look at them, the bobby dazzler girls, and I think, how did you learn to be like that? Where did you get the courage? I didn't have a minute, a second in my life when I felt a bit like that and I wish I had, Lionel. I wish I'd worn those boots and those clothes and that face for half a minute of my life. I might have stood a chance.

Lionel We can get you combat gear, Martha. That isn't a problem.

She laughs.

Lionel You're worth a hundred of any one of those girls.

Martha I feel like I'm declining slowly into invisibility.

Lionel But I've come along. With x-ray specs.

Martha But I don't want to sleep with you, Lionel. I can't sleep with you.

Lionel That's okay. We'll dance. And you can let down your lovely locks for me, eh?

Martha Like Rapunzel.

Lionel Yes. Like Rapunzel.

Martha It's very fine, my hair. There's a lot of it. But it's very fine.

Lionel I'll be the judge of that. I'll go and find Elvis.

Martha Yes.

Lionel Wait there. Don't move.

Lionel exits. Martha goes to the mirror, looks at her reflection, tries to pull her dress down to reveal some cleavage, sighs, goes to the hostess trolley, pours herself a very large drink which she drinks in one.
Josie enters.

Josie Martha, have you seen Shelly-Louise? I mean Louise?

Martha No, Mrs Botting.

Josie I don't know what's happening this evening, Martha. My house seems to have turned into the Bermuda Triangle.

Martha I'm glad you're here, Mrs Botting, because I need to talk to you.

Josie I need to find my daughter.

Martha It really won't take very long. You see, I made a surprising discovery earlier this evening.

Josie Oh?

Martha Concerning the precise nature of the counselling services that you offer here.

Josie I see.

Martha On acquiring this information, I was of course forced to hand in my notice.

Josie Yes. Fine. I'll write you a reference but if you're expecting an apology, you're out of luck. I think I have every right to sweep my life under the carpet, if I want to.

Martha You're right. In any case I've decided to retract my notice. I need to avail myself of your services.

Josie What?

Martha The thing is – I need your advice. Some tips. Just the basics.

Josie I'm not with you.

Martha You see I haven't – I've never, I mean even with Gene Pitney, it never got further than my girdle . . . to tell you the truth, I'm scared out of my wits, Mrs Botting. I'm starting all this from the wrong place.

Josie Now slow down, Martha. What are you saying?

Martha Mrs Botting, Josie, there's a man out there and he's small and he has no hair and he's Jewish and he likes to feel the swirl of air between his legs when he's wearing a dress and I don't know what to do about him.

Josie Lionel?

Martha I think I'd like to become a fallen woman. But I need some lessons.

Josie Well, well, well.

Martha I'm forty-six, and I don't know who else to ask.

Josie Come on then. We'd better have a master-class.

Martha You'll help me?

Josie Come with me. When I've finished with you, he'll think he's died and gone to heaven.

Josie and Martha exit upstairs. At the same time, Brenda-Marie enters from outside with the Chinese Elvis and Lionel trailing behind her, carrying various bits of her tent.

SCENE SEVEN

Brenda-Marie Come on, you two. Lionel, don't lag.

Lionel Martha?

Brenda-Marie I think we'll have it over here in this corner. I can't believe me Mam and me sister haven't come looking for me. But if my tent's right under their noses, there'll be no excuses.

Lionel She's gone. I don't believe it.

Brenda-Marie Lionel, where are you going? You've got to help me and Elvis put my tent up.

Lionel You kept me out there too long and now she's slipped through my fingers.

Brenda-Marie Who?

Lionel Martha.

Brenda-Marie Holy Jo? She's probably looking for suspicious-looking cars.

Chinese Elvis Or else she's done a runner. I know I'd like to.

Lionel Yeah, thanks very much, Elvis. Well, I'm not letting this happen.

He exits upstairs.

Brenda-Marie Lionel! My tent!

Chinese Elvis We'll put it up, Brenda-Marie, don't worry. Here, it's easy. This bit goes in this bit. We'll have this up in no time. Are you going to help me with this?

Brenda-Marie I'll give you directions. You can build it round me.

Chinese Elvis Thanks very much.

He starts to put the tent together. Louise appears. She is back in her ordinary clothes, with her bag, ready to go.

Louise Can I help?

Brenda-Marie It's all right, thank you very much.

Louise Well you look as though you need some help, Elvis.

Chinese Elvis It depends what you mean by help.

Louise It's all right. I'm not going to tie you up or anything.

She puts her bag down and they start to build the tent around Brenda-Marie.

Louise Brenda-Marie, I just wanted to –

Brenda-Marie I'm sorry, I'm very busy right now.

Louise Oh. Okay.

Chinese Elvis Just pass me that bit, Louise. Thanks.

Pause.

Brenda-Marie And here we are in the Heidelburger Stadium. It's minus about a hundred degrees outside. But here's the Botting Sisters from Bolton. They're sure to warm our cockles. And their free programme is going very well with just the desired amount of elements in it. And there's the flying split triple twist which has become their trademark. And now the triple flip. They really flipped their cherries there. And now Brenda-Marie launches into the forward outside death spiral. She's controlling it on her heel. Shelly-Louise has her by the hand. Her head is skimming the ice. Beautiful. But, oh no! Shelly-Louise has lost her grip. She lets her go. Brenda-Marie's head smashes into the ice. She can't control it. Her skull is sliced in two. The ice is turning red. She's lying on the ice. She's not moving.

Chinese Elvis She's dead.

Louise Brenda-Marie –

Louise goes to sit in the frame of the tent with Brenda-Marie, while the Chinese Elvis continues to construct the tent.

Brenda-Marie Barry Davies is crying. He says no-one will ever take her place.

Louise I'm sorry I went away.

Brenda-Marie Barry Davies is a mess. He's got snot running down his face.

Louise I didn't think what it would do to you.

Brenda-Marie Barry Davies was secretly in love with Brenda-Marie Botting from Bolton.

Louise I didn't think I could ever come back.

Brenda-Marie Barry Davies is in tatters.

Louise But I didn't stop thinking about you.

Brenda-Marie Barry Davies has collapsed.

Louise I thought about you every day.

Brenda-Marie They're taking him away in an emergency ambulance. That's the end of his commentating career.

Louise I don't expect you to understand why I did it.

Brenda-Marie Poor Barry Davies.

Louise But I want you to know that it was very necessary.

Brenda-Marie You had to find yourself, I know.

Louise (*surprised*) What? Yes, yes I did.

Brenda-Marie Some people can find themselves just sitting in a tent and some people have to go round pretending they're dead. It's very inconvenient but some people just have to do it.

Louise I didn't pretend I was dead. Mam only said that to make it easier.

Brenda-Marie It didn't make it easier. How could it make it easier?

Louise I'm sorry, Brenda-Marie.

Brenda-Marie Some people think that just by changing their name people will start treating them different. But that's a load of cobblers.

Louise Yes, you're probably right.

Brenda-Marie I think you'll find I am right. I was born with ancient wisdom, you see.

Louise Who told you that?

Brenda-Marie A Chinese acquaintance of mine. The Chinese, you know have the reputation of being very serious thinkers.

Chinese Elvis There we go. That's the frame up.

Louise It's so good to see you, Brenda-Marie.

Chinese Elvis Shall I cover you up now?

Brenda-Marie No, we'll do that, Timothy Wong. You have a rest in my tent now, you've worked very hard.

The Chinese Elvis sits in the tent while they put the canvas over it.

Louise Do you remember what Mam said about the night we were born?

Brenda-Marie It was cold, cold, icicles everywhere.

Louise And she thought there was only one of us.

Brenda-Marie And Shelly-Louise popped out quick as you like.

Louise Like shelling peas.

Brenda-Marie She had no hair. She were a baldy.

Louise And then they said,

Brenda-Marie 'Hang on a minute, there's another one in here!'

Louise But Brenda-Marie wasn't coming out.

Brenda-Marie No, she was staying put. Heave Ho!

Louise And they dragged her out, bawling and shouting.

Brenda-Marie (*giggles*) She had loads of hair. Like fur. All over 'er. To keep her warm.

Louise She was the big surprise.

Brenda-Marie (*delighted*) A bonus baby. Two for the price of one!

Louise But she wasn't a big surprise to me. Because I always knew she was there. Before Mam knew even. That's why I was never lonely. Even when I came out and she stayed put we were never apart.

Brenda-Marie You're going away again, aren't you?

Louise I'm sorry, Brenda-Marie.

Brenda-Marie Don't go.

Louise Some things don't work out the way we want them to.

Brenda-Marie What was the point of coming back if you just go away again?

Louise I tried –

Brenda-Marie You're a bitch.

Louise Brenda-Marie.

Brenda-Marie Go away from me.

Louise I'm sorry.

Brenda-Marie I hate Advent. Because you wait and you wait for the really important person to come and then they come and then they just go away and you have to start waiting all over again, don't you Elvis?

Chinese Elvis Leave me out of this.

Louise Brenda-Marie, maybe I could write to you –

Brenda-Marie Shove over, Elvis. I need to get in. (*She gets into the tent and zips it up.*)

Louise Brenda-Marie?

Pause.

Please.

Louise picks up her bag and prepares to leave. Josie enters from upstairs, behind her.

SCENE EIGHT

Josie Before you go, I want to give you something. (*She hands Louise the snowscene.*) Our Brenda-Marie gave it me this morning. She said if she ever went away that I was to shake it and I'd remember her. And I thought I wish I'd had one of these when our Shelly-Louise left. I'd have shaken it and shaken it and shaken it till you came home.

Louise goes to speak.

I don't want you to speak. I want you to shake it. And again. I want you to keep on shaking it. Don't let the snow settle. And I want you to listen to me. You don't have to look at me. Look at the snow. And don't stop shaking. Shake it again, that's right. Now it's funny that you should come back today of all days. That's it, keep on shaking. I woke up and thought, 'It's time to call it a day, I've made a mess of it all.' But I wasn't worried because I thought, 'I'm going to get myself frozen.' Cryogenics they call it, I pay an arm and a leg and they suspend my head in liquid nitrogen. At minus one hundred and eighty six degrees. Then some time in the next millennium, hopefully they'll have the scientific nouse to thaw me out and wake me up and I can start my life all over again. Keep on shaking. And I thought that would suit me down to the ground. I'll wipe this life out and have another go. And then you came back. And

I realised. I'm already frozen. It happened ten years ago.
My little girl left and I stepped into a casket of dry ice.
I've been suspended in animation for ten years. Living
without hope and without expectations. And then you
came back today. Swap hands, if it's hurting. And I
didn't know what was happening to me. I felt this
tingling sensation in my fingers. And up me arms. And
slowly throughout this evening I got some feeling back.
Because of this prodigal return. No prodigious return.
This brave and prodigious return. So full of good things
that I can't begin to count them. So that's what I've been
doing, I've been thawing out all evening. And that's a
miracle of modern science. A medical impossibility.
You've defrosted me good and proper. Don't let it stop,
Louise. Keep it falling. By coming back today, you've
filled me with expectation again. And I want to be
expecting you always. And so if you went now, my grief
would fall like snow. I would never, never ever settle.
Because my love for you and Brenda-Marie knows no
bloody bounds. When it comes to love, I'm a Goliath.
I've been practising all my life. I don't care if you're
Shelly-Louise or Louise or Louis the bloody Fourteenth,
you'll never stop me. And if you want to be a bride, I'll
run up the bloody aisle with you. And if you want to be
a lap-dancer, I'll fix you a table. And if you want another
break from me, I'll just keep on snowing till you come
back. So that's it. That's the most I've ever said without
the aid of a whip. You can stop now. Let it settle. Let it
settle.

Pause. They watch as the snow falls.

Josie Does your wrist hurt?

Louise Yes.

Josie I'm getting you in training for married life.

Louise Mam –

Josie I know.

Louise I've never –

Josie I know.

Louise I really –

Josie I know.

Louise It won't be all plain sailing.

Josie I know. I know that. Come here.

Josie and Louise embrace. Brenda-Marie appears out of the tent.

Brenda-Marie Will you be able to stay now, Shelly-Louise?

Josie We'll see how it goes, Brenda-Marie. And her name is Louise now.

Louise It's all right, Mam. I don't mind.

Brenda-Marie I hope it snows. I hope it snows so I can catch my death. I want to catch my death so that I can come back like Audrey Hepburn. And everyone can love me all over again. But I've been waiting and waiting all day and there's been no snow for me. It's just not fair, Mam.

Josie I know it isn't, love.

Brenda-Marie Have you found her space in your heart again, Mam?

Josie Yes, love.

Brenda-Marie I'll have to shove over.

Josie No you won't. I've improved my capacity.

Brenda-Marie How do you do that?

Josie Deep breaths, love.

Brenda-Marie takes a deep breath.

We're gonna have to go and see about this Sky Television, aren't we?

Brenda-Marie Yeah.

Josie Why don't you show our Louise what I made you for Christmas?

Brenda-Marie Okay.

Josie Go and put it on then.

Louise Shall I come and help you?

Brenda-Marie No, wait here. I want it to be a surprise.

She exits.

Josie (*suddenly incredulous*) What the – ? What's she brought this tent indoors for?

Louise I think she felt she was missing all the action.

Josie Well, we can't have it in here, cluttering everything up.

Louise (*whispers*) I think Elvis is in there.

Josie Lord above, what's he up to in there?

Louise I think he's in hiding.

Josie goes to the tent, knocks on it.

Elvis, are you in there, love?

Chinese Elvis Yes.

Josie Are you all right?

Chinese Elvis Yes thank you.

Josie I think we've been a bit much for him this evening. Why don't you come out and give us a song, love?

Chinese Elvis I'm keeping my head down for a while.

Josie Oh go on, Elvis.

Chinese Elvis I'd rather not. I'd like to keep myself to myself if it's all the same to you.

Josie We were really hoping for a finale from you.

Chinese Elvis I've lost my voice.

Josie Well. We'll give you a minute to find it.

SCENE NINE

Lionel enters looking very glum.

Lionel Josie. (*He sits.*)

Josie And look at the face on him. What's up, Lionel love?

Lionel She's barricaded herself in the bathroom. She won't talk to me.

Josie Martha?

Lionel I thought I'd won her, Josie.

Josie But you hardly know her, Lionel.

Lionel Why won't she talk to me?

Josie She's probably busy with the Ajax. Caterpillars don't become butterflies overnight, Lionel.

Lionel I've made a fool of myself.

Louise No you haven't.

Josie You've stuck your neck out is all. It's good to do that once in a while.

Martha calls from off.

Martha Josie!

Lionel I'd better go.

Josie You just sit tight, Lionel love. I've got a surprise for you.

Louise You're full of surprises tonight, Mam.

Josie They're a speciality of mine, love.

She goes to see Martha, just off.

Louise I might be getting married.

Lionel Good for you.

Louise It's not definite.

Lionel No. It never is.

Pause.

Where's Elvis?

Louise He's in the tent.

Lionel I think you've got the right idea, Elvis.

Chinese Elvis (*from inside tent*) This evening has bruised my confidence, Lionel.

Lionel You're lucky it's only your confidence.

Josie re-enters.

Josie Lionel. Are you ready?

Lionel What?

Josie It's your birthday. And Christmas. Come at once.

Lionel What?

Josie Come on in, Martha.

SCENE TEN

Martha enters. She is wearing a low cut sexy Spanish flamenco dress. Her hair is tied at the nape of her neck, but with most of it flowing. She has a flower in her hair. Chinese Elvis pops his head out of the tent.

Chinese Elvis Bloody hell.

Josie Miss Delphine used to favour the Spanish look. I thought Martha would be of a similar height. A few nips and tucks and we've worked wonders. Cat got your tongue, Lionel?

Lionel I – I – I –

Josie Elvis has declined to sing, Martha, but I'm ready with the gramophone.

Martha Thank you, Josie. Josie's given me a master-class. She's a very good teacher.

Josie Best in the business, me. I haven't taught her everything I know, there wasn't time. But she'll certainly be able to tickle your fancy, Lionel.

Chinese Elvis Bloody hell.

Josie Go ahead, Martha.

Martha Lionel. I don't want you to say anything. The time for words is past. I want you to dance with me. Josie, if you'd do the honours.

Josie Delighted.

She puts a record on. It is 'One Night' by Elvis

Presley. Martha dances provocatively up to Lionel (very flamenco).

That's it, Martha love. Show him who's boss.

Then she sweeps him off his feet. They dance a 'tango' or something approximating to it. Martha leads and Lionel has trouble keeping up with her. They constantly swap male and female roles. Perhaps it finishes with Lionel leaning backwards in Martha's arms. Josie and Louise watch. Even the Chinese Elvis sticks his head out of the tent.

Well, we know who's going to be wearing the trousers.

Martha Lionel Trills, your head is shining like a Cox's Orange Pippin.

Josie So it is.

Martha I have a real urge to lick your bald head.

Louise Do it, Martha.

Josie Yes but do it front to back, Martha, it's more hygienic.

Martha Stand back please.

Martha licks Lionel's head from front to back.

Martha I could stimulate your follicles, Lionel Trills.

Chinese Elvis Bloody hell.

Louise He's gone very quiet. Are you all right, Lionel?

Josie You've taken the wind right out of his sails, Martha.

Martha Lionel?

Louise He's in love.

Josie He's all shook up.

Lionel (*à la Elvis*) Ah ho ho ho ho yeah yeah yeah.

Josie This Elvis thing. It must be catching.

Louise (*at window*) Oh Mam, look it's started to snow.

Josie So it has. Let's go outside.

Louise Yes.

Lionel (*to Martha*) Take your shoes off, bobby dazzler. I'm taking you for a run.

Martha Oh Lionel, lead me astray!

He helps her take her shoes off.

Louise Come on then.

She runs outside. Josie watches her.

Josie Did I tell you two? I'm expecting again.

Lionel At your age, Josie!

Josie I know, it's a bloody miracle.

Martha Mazeltov, Josie! It couldn't happen to a nicer woman.

Lionel Come on. Let's get snowed on.

They exit. Brenda-Marie enters. She is wearing a replica of Jane Torvill's dress from Ravel's 'Bolero' dance. She rushes in, then seems deflated that no-one is here.

SCENE ELEVEN

Brenda-Marie Mam? Shelly-Louise?

Chinese Elvis Hello.

Brenda-Marie Elvis. What you doing still in my tent?

Chinese Elvis It's safe in this tent. This is the safest place in the house. We should have brought it in sooner. You look – nice.

Brenda-Marie This is me Bolero dress. Me Mam made it for me.

Chinese Elvis You look like – (*He can't quite put a name to it.*)

Brenda-Marie No I don't. Because I can't really dance you see. On the ice. I made that up.

Chinese Elvis Well, nobody wants to hear my Elvis impersonations. 'Cos I'm shit at them.

Brenda-Marie No. The thing is Elvis, we all know you can do Elvis, now we want to hear you sing like Timothy Wong.

Chinese Elvis Timothy Wong can't sing.

Brenda-Marie I bet he can. I bet he's never tried.

Chinese Elvis No.

Brenda-Marie Come on, do it for me now.

Chinese Elvis I can't.

Brenda-Marie Nobody's listening. I'll tell you if you're shit. I'll throw my pants at you. Come on.

Chinese Elvis I'm sorry, Brenda-Marie. I've had enough tonight. I'm not a performing seal.

Brenda-Marie Prima donna.

He zips up the tent. She thinks for a minute. Then she stands up. She addresses the tent.

Brenda-Marie Ladies and gentlemen, I'd like to introduce to you, Mr Timothy Wong. He used to be a

Vietnamese boat boy, but now he's a poofter living in Whalley Range.

The Chinese Elvis unzips the tent –

Chinese Elvis What?

Brenda-Marie His name is Timothy Wong. He hasn't sold any records. His name is Timothy Wong. He hasn't made any films. His name is Timothy Wong. His is the story of raw talent and unbelievable stage whatsit rising from humble beginnings as an Elvis impersonator. His name is Timothy Wong and he's my friend and he's appearing for one night only in my tent in my front room.

Pause.

Brenda-Marie His name is Timothy Wong –

Chinese Elvis All right. All right. We know what his name is.

He begins to sing in his own voice. He starts off tentatively and gains in confidence as he sings. Brenda-Marie gives him a hand to get out of the tent. At the same time he sheds his Elvis layers down to just a tee-shirt and shorts.

Chinese Elvis
Oh I wish I was in the land of cotton
Old time's there are not forgotten –

Brenda-Marie And he's brilliant. You're brilliant, Timothy Wong! You're better than Elvis.

Chinese Elvis
Look away, Look away, look away Dixieland –

Brenda-Marie Sing it, Timothy Wong! (*She begins to dance. She kicks her feet awkwardly. She's quite clumsy.*)

Chinese Elvis
    Oh I wish I was in Dixie
    Hooray, hooray!
    In Dixieland I'll take my stand
    To live and die in Dixie

    *Slowly, slowly her arms lift gracefully and this
    becomes an 'ice-dance'.*

Brenda-Marie Oh bloody hell. It's coming. Mam. It's
coming. The ice-dance is welling up inside me.

Chinese Elvis
    In Dixieland's where I was born –

Brenda-Marie Mam! I'm ice-dancing. I'm doing all the
tricks, Mam.

    During this, the others walk back in and watch her.

Chinese Elvis
    Early on one frosty mornin' –

Brenda-Marie One minute I'm the Torvill. Next minute
I'm the Dean. And where's Barry Davies when you need
him?

Chinese Elvis
    Look away, look away, look away Dixieland.

Brenda-Marie Mam, I'm cutting the ice in swathes.
Look at my patterns. Nobody else can make the patterns
like mine! I'm wearing the see-through tights and the big
pants and I am queen of the ice!

Josie You are.

Chinese Elvis And I can sing!

Lionel He can. He bloody can.

Brenda-Marie And my sister's a bride!

Lionel And so are you, Brenda-Marie.

At the word bride, Josie, Martha and Lionel start to throw handfuls of confetti in the air. The first 'Glory, Glory, Alleluias' in the original Elvis version of 'An American Trilogy' are heard. The confetti starts to fall from the ceiling too. Brenda-Marie continues to dance. Perhaps the lights on the Christmas decoration start to twinkle.

Brenda-Marie And it's snowing, Mam! That's amazing. It's snowing in the house.

Martha Look at the mess!

Lionel Leave it, Martha. We love the mess.

Martha One, two, three, four, five –

Lionel No, Martha, no. Let it fall. Let the snow fall.

Martha One, two, three, four, five –

Louise Yes let it settle.

Martha One, two, three, four, five –

Josie Old habits die hard, Lionel.

Brenda-Marie No, she's trying to say something. I know what she's trying to say.

Martha One, two, three, four, five –

Brenda-Marie Say it Holy Jo! Say it!

Martha One, two, three, four, five –

Brenda-Marie She's judging me. She's giving me my marks!

Martha Six!

Chinese Elvis Technical merit.

Lionel Halleluiah!

Martha Six!

Louise Artistic presentation.

Josie I don't believe it!

Martha Six! Yes!

Brenda-Marie I did it, Mam! I did it! I got the perfect number!

She spins and spins in her final move. The others watch, rapt. The 'snow' continues to fall. The fairy lights twinkle. The final 'Glory, Glory, Alleluiahs' in 'An American Trilogy' play.
    Blackout.